KNACK
MAKE IT EASY

BODY LANGUAGE

KNACK

BODY LANGUAGE

Techniques on Interpreting Nonverbal Cues in the World and Workplace

Aaron Brehove

Photographs by Roger Paperno

Guilford, Connecticut
An imprint of Globe Pequot Press

Copyright © 2011 by Morris Book Publishing, LLC

Editorial Director: Cynthia Hughes
Editor: Katie Benoit
Project Editor: Tracee Williams
Cover Design: Paul Beatrice, Bret Kerr
Interior Design: Paul Beatrice
Layout: Kevin Mak
Cover design: Elizabeth Kingsbury
Cover art: © Shutterstock
Interior Photos by Roger Paperno with the exception of those listed on page 222.

The following manufacturers/names/logos appearing in *Knack Body Language* are trademarks:
Apple®; Botox®; Chronicle Books®; Clorox®; CNN®; Crystal Cruises®; Facebook®, FedEx®, Gap®; Norwegian Cruise Line®; Post-it®, PowerPoint®, Robovie®; Saturn®; Toyota®

Library of Congress Cataloging-in-Publication Data

Brehove, Aaron.
  Knack body language : techniques on interpreting nonverbal cues in the world and workplace / Aaron Brehove ; photographs by Roger Paperno.
    p. cm.
  Includes index.
  ISBN 978-1-59921-949-3
  1. Body language. 2. Nonverbal communication. 3. Nonverbal communication in the workplace. I. Title.
  BF637.N66B74 2011
  153.6'9—dc22

                        2010041108

Printed in China

10 9 8 7 6 5 4 3 2 1

This work is dedicated to my parents, James and Ellen Brehove, whose patient guidance planted the seeds for my successes today.

Acknowledgments

I would like to thank everyone that helped make this book a reality. Without their assistance and support this book would not have been possible.

Daniela Schirmer was my right hand and critical at every step of this process. She consistently went above and beyond, especially in her work on chapters: *Past, Present, Future, Babies, Battle of the Sexes, Proxemics, Cultural Cues,* and *Hands-on Exercises*. I want to thank Shadi Gholizadeh for her work on chapters, *Legs & Feet, Proxemics, Dating & Mating, Seating Arrangements*, and *Selling Yourself*. Thank you to Kalia Simpson, for her work with chapters, *Conscious & Unconscious, Calibrating, Noggin News, Interview Process*, and *We Should Have Seen It*. Thank you to Sydney Tichenor for her help with the chapters on *Clustering* and *Arms & Hands*; Jake Currie for his assistance with the chapter on *Props*; and Thomas Hunt for his contributions to *Hands-on Exercises*. For their practical help in the early research for this book, I would like to thank Christopher Kobes and Regina McFarland. For their assistance with the interviews in *Body Language in Practice,* I'd like to thank Aliza Becker, Evelyn Bourne, Jennifer Wilson, Joe Mullich, and Gwen Parks. I'd like to specially thank Katie Benoit for reaching out to me to write this book.

I cannot forget to thank some of the people that have had a pivotal impact on my professional life, Nancy French-Gerlach, Chuck Owens, Barb Lambert, Traci Allen, Steve Clark, Scott Flemming, Cheryl Hyder, Dan Lentz, and Mike Sherrod.

I am most sincerely grateful to Janine Driver for all of her help and encouragement with the book. She inspired me to take the book in a direction that would be engaging and valuable to readers. Janine changed the trajectory of my life by bringing me into this industry, and she is always pushing me to take the next step in my work and in my personal life.

CONTENTS

INTRODUCTION

There are some events in life that simply change the course you're on and open your eyes to the true path your life should take. Here is the event that steered me on the path to study and fully understand body language:

On February 28, 2004, approximately two hours before the sun came up, my life was changed forever. My head and shoulders pulled back as far as possible, my back arched, and my torso and feet quickly flipped my body at least once. It took less than ten seconds to complete the perfect back flip. Except there was no diving board. No water. No pool. Instead, I flipped off of a second story apartment balcony and my landing pad was the cement sidewalk below.

I spent the next month in and out of the ICU fighting for my life, nearly dying three times. Temporarily paralyzed due to swelling from a compressed vertebra, I was told I would never walk like a normal person again, if at all.

After about a week in the hospital and already nearly dying once due to medication complications, I needed an emergency—but what was expected to be a relatively routine—surgery to release the pressure from the swelling in my back to hopefully stop the progression of my paralysis.

I nearly died on the operating table.

Thankfully, the doctors were able to keep me alive with their skill and technology, putting me on life support and in a drug-induced coma. I awoke from my surgery days later, finding my hands bound to my hospital bed and a tube pushed down my throat to breathe for me. With both legs, ankles, and feet broken, and with a broken pelvis and back, I was in the worst physical pain I had ever experienced in my life.

I soon, however, discovered a pain that would eclipse all other pain: It was while I lay bound and gagged in this

hospital bed that I discovered that not having the ability to communicate brought me more pain and anguish than anything else. It was at this point that my journey to understand all I could about communication began.

A Second Sign

A little over a week later, and still in the ICU, I would experience yet another event that became the catalyst for my life's future work. This time I would be awake for the event.

Around two in the morning I woke up to clear my throat and lungs, as I had to do frequently. This time, however, I began to choke. Within seconds of hitting the panic button, ten doctors, nurses, and paramedics flooded my room, trying to help me breathe, but to no avail. As they looked in my throat they could not see any obstruction or reason why I was not breathing. I began to turn blue, and looked up helplessly at a nurse that I had become very close with. There, registered on her face, I saw something that no patient wants to see: a frozen look of despair. The fight for my life dragged on seemingly hopelessly, and as I lay there amongst the chaos of that hospital room, I experienced what I thought were certainly the last seconds of my life.

Yes, they were merely seconds, but they seemed to last forever. As I reviewed the events of my life, a thought that would change me forever crept into my head. I thought to myself that this world, my community, my friends, my family were not worse for my membership in them, but, rather, the world was a better place because of my participation in it. This thought alone allowed me to say goodbye to my family and friends.

I said goodbye to my life and felt myself starting to slip away.

Back in the chaos, and unbeknownst to me, a paramedic discovered the source of my inability to breathe: a golf ball-size piece of blood and scar tissue lodged in my airway. As I convulsed for the last time, this paramedic saved my life by sticking a small tube up my nose and tweaking it at just the right second to clear my airway and allowed me to breathe again.

I was alive.

And with life, I made a promise to myself: If I was ever again in the position to review my life I would once again be able to say that this was a better world for my participation in it.

During my time in the hospital, my inability to communicate—and that feeling of being trapped in my own body—was the catalyst that led me to fully study, understand, and teach body language. I learned how strong my own body language could be when my voice and other traditional means of communication failed me. In one particular instance in the hospital, a visiting doctor from my psychology team told me that he could see something in me that reminded him of his own self: A young, energetic, and enthusiastic guy. Through my body language he could see that the light in me was not extinguished but rather shining brighter than ever, and it was this man's faith in me that made me fight so hard for my full recovery. Over the years since, as I have learned about it, it has become apparent that a better understanding of body language is a tool that can change your life, and it has changed mine.

Body Language and You

Perhaps you came to read this book because of a general interest in body language. Perhaps you want to use body language to improve your standing in your workplace, master an interview, or even go on a successful first date. Or perhaps, like me, you felt a stronger, maybe higher, calling to

immerse yourself in the study of body language. Regardless, this book will take you through gestures and body language typical of people in the western culture and through some of the differences seen throughout the world. While there are a number of separate sciences that contribute to body language, you will see that this book is a combination of them all.

In these pages, we will cover a number of topics together, and hopefully once you have finished the book you will take away a few key points, pocket a new ability to understand how you are perceived by others, and learn how to read people more efficiently. You should find that, when interacting with someone, no one gesture specifically means anything, but when grouped together with a number of signs and gestures their meaning will seem to be apparent.

The specific gestures of body language are constantly changing, but one of the things that will never change is that, if you think about body language and how it makes you and other people feel, you will become better at understanding it. I hope this book aids you in your quest, whether

it is climbing the corporate ladder or simply developing an environment of better communication between you and your family and friends. I hope, like it did with me, the awareness of body language changes your life for the better.

HISTORY & SCIENCE

Before mastering body language, learn to understand it from many perspectives and fields of study

Body language derives from a combination of what we are already born with and what we experience in our daily lives. Merging science and culture, this form of nonverbal communication is studied and explored in many contexts.

Anthropologists observe its use by humans on an evolutionary level. They might say that our capability to use gestures is genetic or that the way we show emotions on our faces is universal around the world. They may also track how the use of body language transforms through the centuries, across cultures, and in light of historical events.

Sociologists approach body language as a factor that both influences and is a product of human interaction, studying

Stone Age Caveman

- One hundred thousand years ago, our ancestors could not speak.

- Gestural Theory posits that body language preceded spoken language in prehistoric times.

- Scientists believe that after the brain and larynx developed enough in the ancestors of *Homo sapiens*, gesture began to be combined with speech.

- We inherited primal instincts, and corresponding primal gestures remain with us today.

Ancient Romans' Thumbs Down

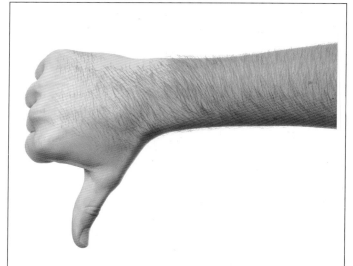

- The thumb gesture originated in ancient Rome.

- The lives of the gladiators depended on this "ultimatum" of the thumb given by the caesar and the crowd.

- Anthropologists still debate which position of the thumb meant death in ancient Rome, but today thumbs up in the United States is celebratory, whereas thumbs down is critical or insulting.

- *Pollice verso* is Latin for this gesture, meaning "a turned thumb."

how it affects society. The way we communicate with our bodies, consciously or unconsciously, can reflect who we are, where we come from, even how much money or power we have.

Body language is pivotal. It changes minds, and it changes history. Just think of how groundbreaking television was because it did what the radio could not do: bring faces to voices. The masses gained a broader worldview; by being able to watch public figures in real time on TV, for example, they could see what was not explained by words alone—emotions, lies, looks, and status, to name a few.

Snob Moves

- An elite person might have some snobby traits, which he uses to display his superiority.

- He may sit with tightly crossed legs, purse his lips, and not give eye contact to someone whom he believes is his inferior.

- Body language can reveal socioeconomic standing.

- Sociologists know how hierarchical structures of power, wealth, age, or education in society affect body language.

Kennedy/Nixon Debates, 1960

- The televised presidential debates exemplify how body language affected voters' opinions and made history.

- Richard Nixon was sweating, giving the appearance of nervousness, whereas John F. Kennedy used eye contact to show his conviction.

- Kennedy's suit matched the set, and he wore makeup. Nixon, not blessed with youthful good looks, appeared ill and refused makeup.

- Many who heard the debate on radio were convinced that Nixon had won, whereas those who watched it on TV believed that Kennedy had won.

1

BODY LANGUAGE GRAMMAR: KINESICS

Kinesics is the study of body movements in relation to communication

The movements and stances of our bodies such as posture, gestures, and facial expressions are usually not random. Put into context, they can have remarkably precise meanings. Together they constitute a nonverbal language.

Ray Birdwhistell, a 1950s anthropologist, proposed kinesics as a field to address the interpretation of body language. Like grammar, kinesics formalizes body language by categorizing types of movement. It can be used as a method of analysis in many scenarios, including lie detection.

For proof that "kinesic movements" exist, get into a car (preferably during rush-hour traffic) and observe other drivers. Unable to communicate verbally, they will exaggerate their body motions to express themselves to each other. Faces contort in emotional, or "affect" display, arms and shoulders move into action to illustrate a message, and hands form emblematic gestures to replace words.

Emblem

- The stop gesture is a widely recognized emblem.

- Emblems substitute for words or phrases and are widely used in sign language.

- Making the stop gesture is not to be confused with raising the hand to swear an oath or to a wave, which vary in degrees of arm extension.

- In some Asian countries, the gesture is not used as an emblem but rather as a regulator (see regulator image at right) to ask for permission to speak.

Illustrator

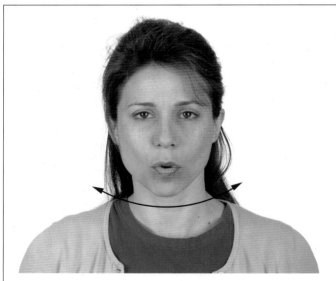

- When we say "no," we often shake the head from side to side illustrating our point.

- Illustrators emphasize or accompany a verbal message or thought.

- When a person makes statements or affirmations and incongruously nods his head "no," it may indicate that he is lying or that he is thinking the opposite of what he is actually saying.

- Other examples of illustrators include shaking our fists when we are angry or slapping our forehead when we make a mistake.

Birdwhistell stressed that specific movements can have multiple interpretations dependent on context. For example, do not assume that a person who is biting his fingernails is nervous. To rule out that it may just be a habit, you must first observe his other body cues to gain more evidence of tension. So, remember that each body movement must be interpreted only in conjunction with other movements and in consideration of social and cultural context.

ZOOM

Affect display, the kinesic category of emotional expression, is most noticeably observed in the face. Some facial expressions are involuntary and occur in a flash of a second. Researchers have identified several of these "microexpressions," and because they cannot be hidden or faked, they can suggest signs of dishonesty or of ulterior motivations. These are further explored on pages 78–81.

Adaptor

- Adaptors, such as biting the nails, are used to relieve tension and are often revealed when people become bored or stressed.

- These behavioral peculiarities are nervous habits or involuntary ticks.

- Other adaptors are touching the hair, fiddling with an object such as twirling a pen, or tapping a desk.

- Do not confuse an adaptor movement with its literal use. A person may just be biting a nail for practical reasons, not necessarily out of nervousness.

Regulator

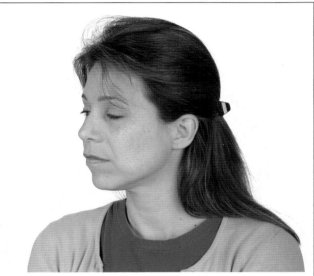

- In some situations when a person turns his head away from a conversation, it may indicate he wants to stop communication or change the subject.

- A regulator controls flow and pace of communication.

- Regulators can be used to direct a conversation or to establish turn taking.

- Other examples include moving away, yawning, and touching someone to initiate an interruption.

MORE NONVERBAL ELEMENTS

You should know a few other categories that influence body language

In addition to the kinesic division of movement types into emblems, illustrators, adaptors, regulators, and affect displays, a couple of other areas of study relate to body language presented in the images below.

When deciphering the meaning of body language, you must note elements other than a person's movements and stance that will affect her actions and influence her presentation and perception.

For example: What clothes is she wearing? What accessories is she using? Many accessories can be used to hide parts of the body—sunglasses, hats, pockets. What are her surroundings, and how does she make use of space? Observe whether

Proxemics

- The individual on the left in the image is "getting in the other person's face," as the expression goes.

- A personal space boundary is aggressively being invaded, and the victim is attempting to move back in order to avoid getting cornered.

- This is an example of a proxemic relation. Proxemics is the study of distances between interacting persons.

- Proxemics reveals comfort zones as well as the type of relationships between people.

Haptics

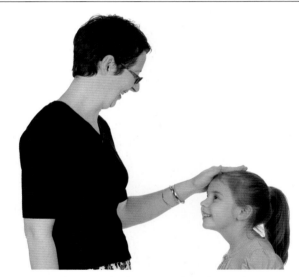

- Haptics is the science of touch. In body language touching can reveal the nature of relationships.

- By patting the child's head, the adult is expressing friendly affection. Although, as this gesture is generally reserved for interaction between an adult and child,

- if used in anohter situation it may have a very different meaning.

- Haptic communication is widely used to greet (such as handshakes), to express sympathy (a gentle touch on the shoulder), and to express friendship and love (hugging and kissing).

or not she moves around a lot in the space or if she stays near the door. How much distance does she keep from another individual? Does she touch other individuals? How does she make use of time in relation to her body language? Are her movements and speech coordinated or awkward and off beat? Is she acting slowly or quickly?

Answering all of these questions will shed light on the specific meaning of a person's body language. These answers will work as additional clues to narrowing the interpretation of a person's message or state of being.

Chronemics

- Chronemics is the study of time. Time itself can be used as a message system.

- Being punctual, pausing, hurrying, waiting, and moving quickly or slowly are examples of time perception.

- Always consider timing of gestures and expressions in accordance with verbal communication. Reaction time reveals much about a person's sincerity.

- Blink rates are an example of chronemics. A person typically blinks fifteen times a minute. The average person blinks between three times a minute while reading and twenty-five to thirty times a minute while speaking. Varying blink rates can be a strong indicator of a change in emotion.

Artifacts

- Our physical accessories many times change the way in which we position our bodies.

- Our body position can project a certain demeanor.

- The phrase "looking down your nose at someone" is a common saying with a known connotation; if you literally look down your nose at someone you may be perceived as arrogant or superior.

- The woman in the image may or may not be aware of the attitude she is projecting because she is looking over the rim of her glasses.

5

BODY LANGUAGE IMPACTS TODAY

Body language is increasingly being noticed, taught, and interpreted in many fields

These days body language professionals are being hired everywhere. How many times have you switched on the television set to see one of these experts analyzing the body signals of a celebrity or politician?

The growing popularity of this field goes to show how important understanding body language is becoming in our world.

It impacts society in all corners: Business, sales, advertising, politics, entertainment, crime detection, and even national security.

You may not know it, but almost every day you probably interact with people who are aware and mindful of what their bodies convey. If you watch TV and movies, you can see actors purposefully using gestures, expressions, and stances.

Detecting Crime

- To keep neighborhoods and communities safe, police must keep an eye out for suspicious behavior.

- Police officers notice suspicious body language and are entitled to search suspects.

- In the court case *Terry v. Ohio* (1968), the Supreme Court ruled that officers can search someone if they have reasonable cause, which includes suspicions raised by body language.

Presenting an Image

- This sign represents the word *okay*.

- Studies have shown that subtly flashing this sign will make an audience more at ease with a presenter's statements or actions.

- This is a common and consistent sign with

similar meanings in English-speaking cultures but very different meanings in other cultures. We will discuss this more in chapter 17.

- The sign originally stood for "all correct," which was incorrectly spelled "oll correct."

The news media rush to analyze body language any time a public figure creates controversy. A salesperson reads your body signals and cues to understand how far to push with his selling tactics. Advertisements harness body language to send a selling message about styles and products. At the airport security guards scan you and every other individual for suspicious behavior. And politicians continuously use body language to enhance their images. Many FBI agents, investigators, and interrogators are professionally trained to spot lies from even the subtlest of body cues.

ZOOM

Body language experts cater to salespeople, executives, and professionals. Many appear as media guests to offer insight into current events. With any prominent speech or memorable meeting among public figures, you can bet that experts are working to decode underlying messages by monitoring each nuance, movement, and expression.

Laugh for Health

- Laughter Yoga is an international health and peace movement started by Dr. Madan Kataria.

- Gathering in groups, individuals maintain eye contact and simulate the body language of joy—smiling and laughter—as therapy.

- It is based on the scientific premise that both real and fake laughter produce the same physiological and psychological benefits.

- This is not a joke! Laughter clubs exist worldwide.

Exaggeration as Entertainment

- The adult in this image is imitating a disgruntled child through stance with toe dug into ground, hands thrust into pockets, and shoulders thrust down.

- Exaggeration of body language is used in entertainment to create comedy and parody.

- Mimes are masters of this art. Charlie Chaplin was one of the most popular actors in silent films because of his hilarious gestures and expressions.

- Today we see actors such as Will Ferrell and programs such as *Saturday Night Live* doing the same thing.

TECHNOLOGY

Take a look at how body language is incorporated into these technologies

Given the popularity of body language as a field of interest these days, we should keep an eye on its present and future developments, especially in the realm of technology as life becomes more high-tech by the day.

As visual and interactive technology increases, we suddenly find camera and video capabilities in every new gadget on the market. This just proves that people want to see each other when they communicate. Being visually present is essential for effective communication because appearance, demeanor, and body language are just as influential as written and spoken words.

Body language influences on technology can also be seen

Video Conferencing

- Some businesses are now using video conferencing to connect with their clients.

- Being able to meet face to face can enhance or solidify relations and collaboration, though it may cause anxiety.

- TelePresence by Cisco is one video conferencing system that uses full-size displays in high definition.

- As gestures, facial expressions, and gaze direction become visible, communication is facilitated.

Avatars

- Avatars are computer-generated representations of a human. These creations use body language to add to their realism and believability.

- In the past to convey messages through body language, developers overstated gestures and body

parts, but as technology advances so does the ability of developers to make avatars appear more realistic by using subtle gestures such as facial movements.

- Avatars play a role in filling the void that people feel because of a lack of human interactions.

in today's cartoons. Have you ever noticed how animated cartoons and anime are more lifelike and realistic? As computer-generated graphic enhancements develop, the cartoonists of the future incorporate minute details of body movement that precisely mimic real humans. Elements of body language are thus enhanced, and characters and storylines become more complex. These days cartoons aren't just for kids. Among other advances, lie detection technology is being developed with machines that measure the diameter of the pupils to check for dilation, which signifies certain states of mind.

YELLOW ● LIGHT

Polygraphs, or lie detector machines, measure vital signs such as heart rate, blood pressure, respiratory rate, and perspiration. These instruments can indicate deceptive behavior but are notoriously unreliable. As neuroscience technology develops, lying will be much more easily exposed. Another technique is thermal imaging, which shows warm spots around the eyes that appear during lying.

Robovie

- Technologies, such as the Robovie, are being developed to delve into the science of body language itself.

- The Robovie robot was used for experiments to study eye contact by Carnegie Mellon University, Japan's Osaka University, and ATR Intelligent Robotics and Communication Laboratory.

- When Robovie looked at two people in a conversation, the individuals took turns speaking.

- If Robovie only glanced at them, they spoke less. If there was no eye contact at all, they did not speak.

- These results were accurate 97 percent of the time.

Botox

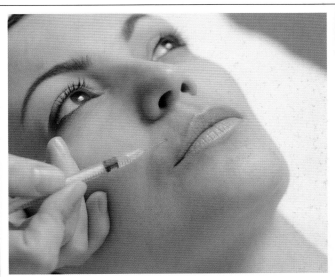

- In the pursuit of a youthful face, Botox leaves a person with an impaired ability to express emotions.

- Studies have shown excessive Botox will harm people's relationships.

- This harm is assumed to be caused by the inability to show "genuine" emotions in the face.

- Mirror neurons are the reason for this detrimental effect of Botox. If people cannot smile strongly, their friends do not react as strongly to this Botox-weakened gesture.

BRAIN MATTERS
One theory regarding evolution of the brain attempts to explain some abilities unique to humans

As evolution progressed from single-celled organisms to humans, the brain developed into one capable of extraordinary comprehension, complex coordination, and high levels of reasoning. Although exceptions to the Triune Brain Theory exist, the theory remains of interest because of its simplicity and power of explanation for many brain structures and functions.

According to the Triune Brain Theory, the earliest structure of the human brain, called the "reptilian brain" because it is posited to be shared with reptiles, is concerned with satisfying our most basic survival needs of food, water, shelter, and sex. Following the progression of evolution, the paleomammalian complex, or limbic system, is considered the

Triune Brain Theory

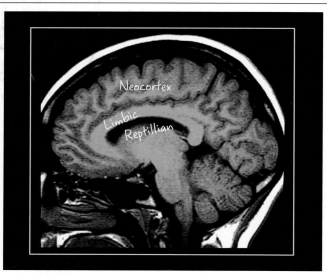

Neocortex
Limbic
Reptillian

- Reptilian complex: The earliest structure, the "primitive brain" regulates self-preservation and aggression.

- Paleomammalian complex (limbic system): Added early in mammalian evolution, the "intermediate brain" controls emotion.

- Neomammalian complex (neocortex): As the most recent evolution, the "rational brain" allows for comprehension and completion of intellectual tasks.

Reptilian Brain

- The reptilian brain regulates instinctual behaviors such as aggression, dominance, territoriality, and ritual displays as well as controls breathing, heart rate, and the fight-or-flight mechanism.

- It is the oldest and smallest portion of the brain, named

"reptilian" because of the early belief that this portion of the brain dominated the forebrain of reptiles and birds.

- It is concerned with achieving our most basic needs of food, shelter, and reproduction.

intermediate portion of the brain that allows for emotion, motivation, and pleasure, all of which impact an organism's characteristic behavior.

We as humans are the only organisms capable of abstract thinking. The field of animal cognition has yet to prove that any other organism is able to imagine the future, think hypothetically, or communicate through the use of a concrete language. This theory suggests that the most recent step in the evolution of the human brain, the development of the neocortex brain, is what allows for these abilities.

The functions of the reptilian brain are automatic and resistant to change. The more advanced limbic system controls emotion. The largest portion of the brain is the neocortex. The two-way connections between the neocortex and the limbic system provide a link between thinking and emotion, furthering the override of instinctual reptilian behavior by voluntary behavior.

Paleomammalian Brain: Limbic System

- The limbic system controls olfaction, long-term memory, and the motivation and emotion involved in parenting.

- The "amygdala" is important in the association of events with emotion as well as anticipation of consequences.

- The hippocampus converts information into long-term memory and creates cognitive maps for navigation.

- The brain's pleasure center, also located here, allows for sexual arousal and the high one gets from recreational drugs.

Neomammalian Complex: Neocortex

- The neomammalian complex is the most recent step in evolution, unique to the human brain.

- Although all mammals have a neocortex, it is relatively small and has few or no folds.

- The human neocortex is about two-thirds of the entire brain's mass and has many folds, allowing for higher thinking such as language, abstract reasoning, and sensory perception.

- Whereas other animals are "stuck in the present," humans are able to imagine future possibilities.

BRAIN POWER
Right/left hemisphere lateralization explains much—but not all—about brain function

The brain consists of a right and a left hemisphere connected by the corpus callosum, which facilitates communication between the two hemispheres. The hemispheres are considered lateralized—controling different modes of thinking and processing of information, termed "creativity versus logic."

Most people are left-brain dominant—concerned with objectivity and accuracy, and auditory/verbal learners. People who are right-brain dominant are concerned with subjectivity and aesthetics, and visual learners. The remaining people are "whole-brained" and do not have hemisphere dominance.

Scientists in the 1940s discovered that stimulation of the right hemisphere's motor cortex produced muscle contraction in

Right Brain

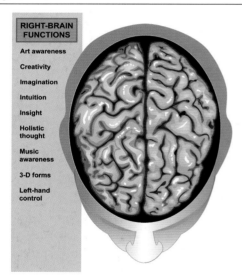

RIGHT-BRAIN FUNCTIONS

Art awareness

Creativity

Imagination

Intuition

Insight

Holistic thought

Music awareness

3-D forms

Left-hand control

- Right-brainers are visual, creative, emotional, and risk-taking and inclined to use gestures.

- Because the right brain controls the left side of the body, a right-brain stroke causes paralysis on the left side of the body (but the right side of the face).

- Right-hemisphere stroke survivors have problematic spatial abilities; loss of depth perception makes walking or driving difficult.

- The individual may have vision problems and memory loss and adopt a quick, inquisitive behavioral style.

Left Brain

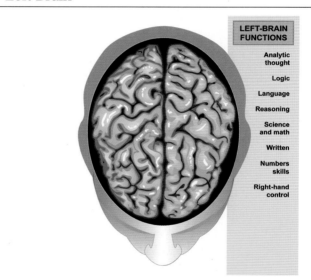

LEFT-BRAIN FUNCTIONS

Analytic thought

Logic

Language

Reasoning

Science and math

Written

Numbers skills

Right-hand control

- Left-brainers are verbal, practical, and safe, plan ahead, and speak with few gestures.

- A left-brain stroke patient will have paralysis on the right side of the body (but the left side of the face).

- Speech and language problems are common in survivors with severity ranging widely.

- The individual may suffer memory loss and adopt a slow, cautious behavioral style, needing much instruction and feedback to finish tasks.

the right side of the face but the left side of the body and vice versa. The idea of lateralization is not absolute and has many exceptions. Much research has been done with individuals with damage to a specific region of the brain, finding that function can be recovered by another brain region, sometimes in the opposite hemisphere. Scientists attempting to map out the brain and provide reasoning behind impaired social functioning have been unsuccessful. As a result, the underlying mechanisms of the various social disorders are largely a mystery.

ZOOM

Communicating with language is made possible by two key regions in the brain. In the left frontal lobe, Broca's area is responsible for speech production; damage to this may impede the ability to speak. In the dominant hemisphere, Wernicke's area hosts the ability to comprehend language. One with damage to this region may lose the ability to understand written and spoken language.

The Social Brain

- Autism is a disorder that affects neural development, resulting in a lack of social and communicative abilities.

- About one-third to one-half of individuals with autism never develop the speech skills necessary to verbally communicate with others.

- Asperger's is a mild form of autism, leaving linguistic and cognitive abilities intact but causing impaired nonverbal communication skills.

- Individuals with Asperger's have trouble understanding emotion, empathizing with others, and using nonverbals—eye contact, posture, and gestures—appropriately.

The Antisocial Brain

- Psychopaths are individuals who can distinguish right and wrong but lack remorse in their purposeful wrongdoings.

- Brain activity of psychopaths during presentation of unpleasant images shows absence of the normal physiological responses to fear.

- Psychopaths are not able to recognize facial expressions of fear and sadness in others but can successfully identify happiness as an expression.

- Brain scans of psychopaths also show impaired functioning in pathways associated with consequences—anticipation of punishment and reward.

NEURAL PATHWAYS

Brain scans reveal intricate mechanisms by which we are capable of cognitive abilities

The guiding principle of body language is that your brain activity and mood affect the way your body behaves. The overall goal of studying body language is to better understand a person's thoughts by analyzing his or her nonverbal cues. Although people can learn to control certain behaviors in an attempt to mask their true feelings, inevitably some clue to the truth will unconsciously leak out.

Law enforcement agencies train their officers to read body language so that they can detect deception. Although polygraph tests can help to determine if a suspect is being untruthful, they require time and training to administer and aren't 100 percent accurate. In fact, it's possible to fool a

Pathological Liars

- Studies of MRIs focusing on the pre-frontal brain reliably found a significant increase in the volume of white matter in the brains of pathological liars compared with those of antisocial and normal control individuals.

- What is not clear is whether the increased volume is pre-existing or induced by long-term repetitive lying.

- It may not surprise you then that researchers have found learning to juggle will increase the amount of white matter in someone's brain.

Gray Matter Matters

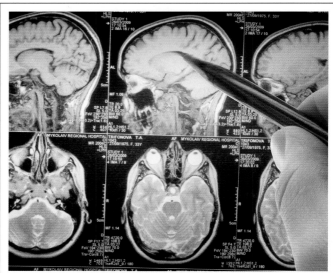

- People with unusually high levels of intelligence tend to have a higher level of gray matter in corresponding parts of the brain.

- While juggling has been shown to increase white matter, Dr. Daniel Amen has produced studies that show a correlation between people who practice judo and a significantly higher gray matter concentration.

- The more gray matter you have, the more brain cells there will be, and in turn the better brain function.

polygraph. Ongoing research into the neural mechanisms of lying, which cannot be faked or covered up, makes true lie detection an exciting possibility.

In reading this book you may seek to learn a person's unspoken or hidden feelings—nervousness, anger, sadness, interest, and so forth. These emotions often manifest themselves physically, allowing you to spot them (if you know what to look for). Although you will learn that body language has no absolute meaning, you can look for multiple signs—or "clusters"—and use your knowledge to interpret them.

ZOOM

"Fake it 'til you make it" is a well-known theory that suggests that the more positive body language you use, the more happiness you will feel. One study found that in patients with major depressive disorder, smiling in the mirror for twenty minutes each day was actually more effective than taking antidepressant medications.

CONSCIOUS & UNCONSCIOUS

Negativity Hurts

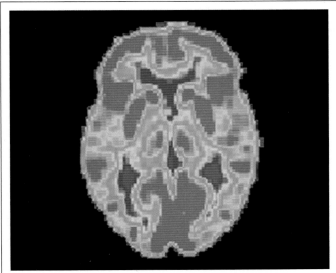

- It has been shown that anxiety, negativity, and depression are commonly the result of brain dysfunction. It has also been shown that allowing these issues to fester will promote more significant dysfunction.

- These dysfunctions typically occur in the deep limbic system and left temporal lobe.

- Through SPECT (Single Photon Emission Computed Tomography) we can see marked improvement almost immediately after starting treatment.

Person in Love

- Dr. Helen Fisher has done brain imaging of people who say they are "madly in love" and found activity in the area of the brain that produces the neurotransmitter dopamine.

- Surprisingly this would support the common phrase "weak in the knees." Norepinephrine, a stress hormone that governs attention and responding actions, makes you weak in the knees. Norepinephrine and dopamine are closely related.

- Dr. Winnifred Cutler and colleagues at the University of Pennsylvania found that regular (weekly) sexual activity enhances estrogen levels in women and in turn overall brain activity and improves memory.

BRAIN BOOSTS

Take matters into your own hands with simple strategies to improve brain functioning

Dr. Daniel Amen's book, *Change Your Brain, Change Your Life,* gives natural alternatives to prescription medication such as cognitive exercises, healthy brain foods, and healthy ways of thinking. Along with explaining the mechanisms behind the problems of anxiety, depression, obsessiveness, anger, and impulsiveness, Amen describes ways that he and

other scientists have proven effective in conquering these problems.

Research has found that the brain function is affected in many different ways by physical and social actions. Active regions in the brain use significantly more energy than inactive regions of the brain. Although the brain is only about 2

Exercise Emotional Expression

- Public speaking is an artistic performance much like acting; both involve the deliverance of a scripted message with poise, emotion, and conviction.

- Effective actors and orators are trained to show emotion through facial expressions, tone of voice, and body language—even urged to slightly exaggerate movements in order to make the audience feel the same emotional state as the speaker.

- A hormone called "oxytocin" is released when showing emotions and it interacts with other hormones to produce positive feelings.

Exercise Your Brain

- Dr. Daniel Amen's book teaches you that the more you exercise your brain, the stronger your brain will be—just like any other part of your body.

- Along with getting regular sleep and physical exercise, thinking positively and performing cognitive activities can drastically reduce your risk of dementia and Alzheimer's.

- Cognitive exercise includes working logic and crossword puzzles, reading, memorizing facts, and deviating from your normal daily routine—anything that causes your brain to be active.

- You can change your daily routine by rearranging your office or bedroom, using your nondominant hand, or taking a different route to work.

percent of a person's body weight it uses about 20 percent of the body's oxygen consumption. With the knowledge of these facts, it is not surprising that physical exercise can improve cognitive ability.

Researchers have established that the brain works very much like a muscle, in the sense that exercise has a positive effect on ability. There are many different and interesting ways of exercising ranging from altering daily routines to solving crosswords. Just as is true with physical exercise, varying exercises work various muscles, the same is true of the brain, and exercising one area of the brain will have a more significant effect on that specific area of the brain.

Throughout your life people may have told you that eating carbohydrates before a run will help fuel you for the run and eating proteins after lifting will help feed your muscles to grow. We now have found that in a very similar sense the foods we eat have marked effects on our brain function.

Employing a few techniques found in this section will aid you in developing your brain and hopefully your life.

Positive Intake

- Wild salmon: Low in saturated fat and rich in high-quality protein, salmon is one of the best sources for essential fatty acids, improving brain matter and neural connections.

- Chocolate: The cacao bean has most of the health benefits that enhance cognitive function and improve mood. Although candy bars give you a temporary high, the inevitable sugar crash outweighs any brief benefits.

- Blueberries and acai berries: Great sources of antioxidants, essential fatty acids, and even protein.

What to Avoid

- Poor diet: Eating artificial and highly processed foods, colas, high-sugar drinks, white bread, and hydrogenated fats and overeating cause subpar brain functioning.

- Drugs and alcohol: Drugs and alcohol interrupt the normal release of neurotransmitters, which stabilize mood, produce natural euphoria, and carry out many other important functions. Your brain learns to depend on an outside source for these functions and causes withdrawal when the drugs or alcohol is absent.

- Negative thinking.

SUBLIMINAL MESSAGES
Most body language is acted out as well as perceived subconsciously

Although early claims of subliminal messages in records and tapes have been disproven, it's interesting to imagine the implications their existence would bring about: brainwashing, falsified emotions, planted beliefs, and so forth. Although these types of controversial messages designed to bypass consciousness and speak to the subconscious mind

are myths, some environmental stimuli do register without awareness of the conscious mind.

Before you began tuning in to body language, many feelings you got about people were due to intuition. It's likely that the gut feelings were caused by things you observed—posture, facial expressions, tone of voice—without the observations

FedEx's Hidden Message

Individual's Hidden Message

- FedEx is a courier company that has ground and air divisions.

- The creators of the logo purposely placed an arrow between the "E" and "x" as a subliminal message.

- The arrow is said to imply the speed, direction, and reliability of FedEx.

- The body language move pictured is referred to as "hooking"—one or both hands in the pockets with the thumbs sticking out.

- Hooking can also be done by placing one or both thumbs into the pocket with the rest of the fingers sticking out.

- The subliminal message here is in the formation of an arrow with the hands, pointing at the groin region.

- This move exudes confidence in a sexy, attractive way.

"registering" with your conscious mind. You couldn't tell why the man scared you, but you felt fear when he was around.

Much of what your body language says about you is perceived by others without a second thought. People can think of you as an insecure person without first analyzing your posture, how you cross your legs or hold your head.

············· GREEN ● LIGHT ·············

The great thing about body language is that it works both ways—you can learn to better read people while also learning how to portray the traits you want others to perceive of you. When you change your body language to exude confidence, others will pick up on it whether they are knowledgeable about body language or not.

Same Text, Different Interpretations

I love you

I love you

I love you

- Notice how the different fonts change the meaning and tone of the text.

- Script: This careful, neat font was probably written relatively slowly and implies a serious and romantic passion behind the statements.

- Scribbled: This messy and erratic writing was probably written quickly, creating a frantic or impulsive feel and causing you to interpret the statements differently.

- Bubble letters: This font is playful, diminishing the seriousness of the text and making it seem almost childish and harmless.

Same Body Language, Different Interpretations

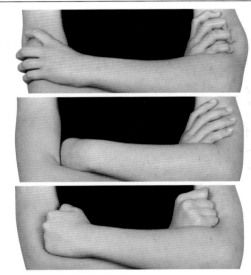

- Just as variations in font can change the meaning of the same text, every body language move can be varied to achieve the meaning you are aiming for.

- Hands clutching arms: This version of the arm cross is perceived as insecurity and makes the individual appear closed off.

- Hands and arms relaxed: This individual still appears closed off but may be simply crossing arms for comfort.

- Fists clenched: This individual appears to be holding back his anger by restraining his clenched fists.

MIND READING: AVOID AT ALL COSTS!
Body language analysis is only a clue—not a way to read thoughts

Our personal thoughts are often the only thing that stay personal. When you tell someone a secret about yourself, you trust that person with that information.

Mind reading is an ability that would change the world. There would be no need for forensics and private investigators, and games like poker would not be too much fun.

When attempting to infer meaning from an individual's body language, know that no move has an absolute meaning. You have to look for clusters of moves that allow you to draw a reasonable hypothesis about the individual's inner thoughts and feelings, at which time you can confront the person about your suspicion with a question. The only way to know how a person really feels is to ask him—and even then he may lie.

If you picked this book up with the goal of becoming a mind reader, stop now. You will not be able to suddenly

Ask Questions

- You'll find that just asking questions of a person will change your interactions and build rapport.

- If you are trying to read someone's body language and it seems that you have offended him, instead of ignoring this or making an assumption, ask if what you've said or done has offended him.

- You will find that a comment or action that may have driven a wedge in your relationship will actually strengthen it because the offended person will feel as though you are concerned with his feelings.

Mind Reading Causes Trouble

- A personal story about the dangers of attempting to mind read:

- While out with friends, I hit it off with a girl and, in an attempt to impress, began vocalizing my assessments of her based on her body language. The girl, amazed at my ability to "read" her, brought her friends over to observe.

- But here's the problem with mind reading: It's impossible to do it correctly, consistently.

- After several correct "reads," I soon lost my touch, and several incorrect "reads" later, I also lost the girl.

understand everyone around you or tell if someone is lying with 100 percent accuracy. What this book will do is give you the tools and information you need to become more perceptive and accurate in your interpretation of the possible meaning behind an individual's body language, at which point you can act accordingly to get the result you are looking for or just ask.

Whose Fault Is It?

- Issues arise when we make assumptions and try to mind read.

- Instead of making assumptions that someone is bored with the conversation, ask him. He may just need a bathroom break.

- A tapping could indicate to you that your friend is anxious to leave, but he may just be cold.

- Ask the questions in the Post-it (at right) to make sure you don't fall into these pitfalls.

Questions to Ask

- If you would actually like to know what someone is thinking, simply ask.

- A common error made by people when asking questions is that they talk too much.

- When trying to gather information you should speak about 20 percent of the time. For example:

  - Is there a reason why...?

  - Tell me about...?

  - How do you feel about...?

THE IMPORTANCE OF BASELINING

Baselining—the evaluation of a person's normal behavior—is essential to understanding body language

The study of body language has been met with much criticism from those who claim that body language means nothing. That is a valid claim. Body language in itself means nothing. You cannot, in fact, determine that someone is lying based on his lack of eye contact.

Think about what you've been told throughout your life about

what body language means and then forget it. Remember that body language *means* nothing until you first determine an individual's baseline. For example, when evaluating eye contact, the meaning comes when an individual deviates from his baseline of intense eye contact to spotty eye contact or vice versa—then you may be on to something.

Compare Baseline with Reaction

- Casual Officer:

- This is the officer's baseline: His weight is over the heel of his rear leg, focus is not intense, and his arms are relaxed.

- Action Officer:

- The photo above shows the

officer in a heightened state of alarm. His body language has changed due to the situation.

- *His footing is strong,* with his focus on something straight ahead, and his arms are ready for action.

Compare Baseline with Reaction

- Prior baseline of woman on the right: Hands were relaxed at sides, head level, eye contact moderate, feet 6 to 10 inches apart, body square to person she talks to.

- Compare the baseline with the current situation in the image: Her body is now

turned away making her appear stand-offish.

- Her arms are tensely pressed against her sides, a sign she could be protecting something.

- She talks with either increased or decreased eye contact.

As mentioned, there is no such thing as a mind reader. You cannot assume you know an individual's thoughts just by looking at certain moves he makes. However, if interpreted effectively, body language has the ability to imply context, mood, and relationships between people. Baselining is the first step toward understanding the function and implications of a person's body language.

Many factors should be taken into account when determining an individual's baseline. This section will teach you those factors and how to use them to better read people.

Determine Your Own Baseline

- To determine your own baseline, stand in front of a mirror with a relaxed, comfortable stance, one that you would assume naturally.

- Head: Do you hold your head slightly tilted to the side? Chin slightly up? Do you look at the ground?

- Shoulders: Are your shoulders back so your chest sticks out? Or are they droopy and conveying a lack of confidence?

- Limbs: Are your arms folded across your chest or comfortably at your sides? How far apart are your feet?

Baseline your own body: A great way to learn to baseline is to practice your skills on your own body language. Doing so helps you to realize what signals you send to others as well as to understand that no body language move has an absolute meaning. Just because you cross your arms doesn't mean you are a closed-off person—you may simply be most comfortable that way.

CALIBRATING

Video Camera Enlightenment

- Borrow or purchase a video camera as an investment in your body language and film yourself in the following three scenarios to get your baseline:

- 1. Watching TV for thirty minutes (set up camera and then forget it's there).

- 2. Having a conversation over a meal or tea with a friend (again, forget about the camera).

- 3. Standing up talking about yourself and your interests for five minutes (no podium—you must see the whole body).

23

BASELINING BASICS

Sharpen your observational skills to allow for the gathering of an accurate, unbiased baseline

Sharpening your observation skills is essential if you hope to understand the science of body language. You need to consider certain variables, such as cultural and situational differences. With respect to cultural variables, for instance, did you know that shaking your head, a gesture that Americans understand to mean "no," actually means "yes" in some Middle Eastern cultures? Or that picking your nose in public is perfectly acceptable in China?

In order to accurately baseline an individual, you must account for more than just possible cultural differences. You also must look at the individual's entire body because some body language moves are subtle and involve only one part

Consider Contrasting Cultures

- Before baselining, take the first three minutes when meeting someone new to consider cultural differences.

- Women from the South are taught to be much more conservative than women from the North and may have a much smaller stance.

- You would be surprised to find out what some of our common gestures mean in other cultures. Take some time to research.

- Eye contact is another body language variable that differs greatly among cultures.

Look at the Big Picture

- Create a setup that allows you to see the person's full body, head to toe.

- In any setting—bar, office, meals, and so forth—minimize barriers or distractions.

- If a barrier such as a table is present, choose to sit in a booth or on a bench, move the table, or sit at a glass table.

- Don't choose a seat where one person can see the TV, and one person's back is to the TV; this arrangement will inhibit communication.

of the body. Besides knowing *what* to baseline, you need to know *when* to baseline. The best time is when the individual is feeling comfortable and relaxed, so you can get a grasp on normal behavior, how he or she acts when alone or not under stress. Lastly, make sure your own body language is promoting an open atmosphere. If a person thinks he is being judged because you are crossing your arms with a discerning look on your face, he is not likely to act naturally.

When attempting to read a person's body language, it is easy to fall victim to something called the "fundamental attribution error." This phrase describes the tendency to attribute observed behavior to a dispositional explanation rather than to account for situational influences. Said plainly, this is when you make an assumption about a person's personality or temperament based on behavior that may actually be situational.

No-pressure Baselining

- The time to baseline is when people are comfortable with one another or are unaware that they are being evaluated.

- After you have baselined someone, you will be able to pick out subtleties that may mean a disagreement, deception, or uneasiness.

- A step back, a crossing of arms, and a turning away slightly could mean deception or disagreement with what you are saying.

- A change in eye contact, fidgeting, and turning away slightly could indicate uneasiness.

Promote an Open Atmosphere

- While gathering a person's baseline, keep your body language open to avoid making the person feel defensive or shy.

- Crossed arms, a lean back, and staring eye contact will not allow you to get an accurate baseline.

- Instead, ask casual, open-ended questions to get the individual comfortable talking.

- When you talk, use palm-up gestures to welcome the person's thoughts and opinions.

CALIBRATING

BODY MOVES TO BASELINE

Practice these four easy steps to become brilliant at baselining anybody

Now that you have set yourself up with the knowledge and an environment that facilitate accurate baselining, you are ready to get going. Baselining someone may seem overwhelming in the beginning; there are so many possibilities in body language, especially when you consider differences because of culture, age, and gender. The now-seemingly overwhelming task of baselining will become second nature with practice. In this section you will learn to HALT:

- **H**eed the head
- **A**ssess the chest
- **L**ook at the limbs
- **T**ake note of the tendencies

Heed the Head

- The head is where a person gathers most sensory information, and how he positions it is important.

- Questions to ask:

- Is the head tilted slightly to the left or right while listening?

- Is the head tilted up, down, or straight ahead while talking?

- When passive, does the person look ahead? Down at his feet or lap?

Assess the Chest

- The shoulders and poise and angle of the body can hint at levels of confidence as well as indicate interest.

- Questions to ask:

- Are the shoulders back and chest out, or are the shoulders slumped?

- Is posture upright, or is the back slumped?

- In conversation is the body angled toward the other party or slightly away?

By following these four steps, you will account for all regions of the body as well as for any repetitive moves you observe for an individual. This process is the same for all individuals you will baseline and ensures that you leave no body language, no matter how small, unnoticed. In the coming week, practice baselining on at least ten people, be it at work, at a friend's house, or at home. Remember the tips discussed previously (considering culture, looking at the big picture, baselining during minimal pressure, and promoting an open atmosphere) to accurately baseline.

Look at the Limbs

- The limbs are extensions of the person; many people find it hard to relax them naturally when nervous.

- Questions to ask:

- Are the arms relaxed by the individual's side? Folded across the chest? Clasped in front of the waist or in the lap? Making gestures?

- When standing, how far apart are the legs? Is the individual leaning to one side?

- When sitting, are the legs crossed? Is one foot up on the knee of the other leg?

Take Note of Tendencies

- Bad habits tend to surface when one is nervous; you must baseline to see if these "nervous ticks" are simply the person's norm.

- Questions to ask:

- Does the individual display self-touch gestures (one part of the body touches another part) such as cracking knuckles, playing with cuticles, and so forth?

- Does the individual have repeated rhythms, such as foot or leg bouncing, hand or fingers tapping?

- Does the individual fidget with things around him?

CALIBRATING

CELEBRITY BASELINES

Follow the same basic rules of baselining when speculating about celebrities

Many celebrity gossip outlets have recently become interested in celebrity body language. These magazines and websites hope to find out who is secretly dating whom or who is hiding what by decoding body language subtleties of people of interest. Many golf fans scrutinized Tiger Woods's body language as he made his public apology on national television and, even before that, when allegations were first brought to light. Brad Pitt's marriage to Jennifer Aniston and his relationship with Angelina Jolie are still constantly being picked apart according to their body language in photographs. Martha Stewart's submissive and ashamed body language during her early-2000s accusation and trial was scrutinized all

Conservative and Matronly

- The norm of conservative celebrities such as Martha Stewart, Diane Keaton, and Oprah Winfrey includes:

- Head: Friendly expression on face, head slightly tilted to the side, chin level.

- Chest: Upright posture, shoulders back.

- Limbs: Conservative, narrow stance, arms relaxed by side when not in use or gesturing.

- Tendencies: Likely no self-touch gestures, repeated rhythms, or fidgeting.

Conservative and Matronly Does a 180

- After baselining a conservative, matronly older woman, you would be surprised to find her acting wildly and provocatively.

- The wild expression on her face is far from the friendly, reserved norm.

- Although the woman is likely to use gestures, the "rocker" pose and provocative dancing are obviously out of character.

- You could conclude that the woman is around close friends and family where she feels comfortable to let loose or has had too much to drink.

over the nation. Although it is fun and entertaining to speculate about what we may or may never know, a key ingredient often is missing in these analyses: The baseline.

Just as you must consider your date's normal behavior before concluding because of crossed legs that he or she is not interested, the same is true with celebrities and their affairs. You already know that mind reading is impossible when it comes to those around you, so why does that knowledge get overlooked when it comes to celebrities? People tend to mind read celebrities because it's easier than

attempting to get an accurate baseline on these individuals, and people like to gossip whether the gossip is true or not. The truth is that baselining celebrities is extremely difficult because the celebrities know they are being watched, or they are actually playing a character in a movie or on TV.

Celebrities are entertaining whether they are acting or not because people love to be fans and to follow their lives. Although it's fun to speculate, you still need to use HALT to break down a celebrity's normal body language first.

Wild and Outgoing

- The norm of outgoing celebrities such as Jenny McCarthy, Lady Gaga, and Kanye West includes:

- Head: Expressive face, chin slightly up; likely to make a facial expression rather than smile in pictures.

- Chest: Upright posture, shoulders back.

- Limbs: Hands on hips, in pockets with thumbs sticking out, or relaxed by side.

- Tendencies: Because of high energy, may display some fidgeting but likely to channel energy into some mindful action.

Wild and Outgoing Does a 180

- After baselining a wild and outgoing individual, you would be surprised to find him or her quietly doing housework or reading in a park alone.

- Although most everyone does these tasks at some point, the individual would likely make noise or move more than necessary while working.

- The individual might be on the phone, singing out loud, dancing, or bouncing a leg.

- You could suppose tiredness, sadness, an otherwise poor mood.

FEAR & ANXIETY

The human body's natural fear mechanism underlies its nonverbal communication of anxiety

Imagine that you have spent weeks preparing for an important presentation at work. As you enter the room, your heart begins to pound, you feel yourself break into a cold sweat, and you feel a little dizzy. Your mouth is parched and dry. After you are up at the podium, your hands shake and fidget. You loudly clear your mucus-lined throat as the first few shaky words begin your presentation. This situation exemplifies a classic case of fear and anxiety. The fidgeting, throat clearing, sweating, dizziness, and dry mouth you experience are but a few examples of fear and anxiety gesture clusters. When we experience stress, our bodies react by secreting stress hormones, such as adrenaline. The brain sends the body a rush

Lip Licking, Paling of the Face

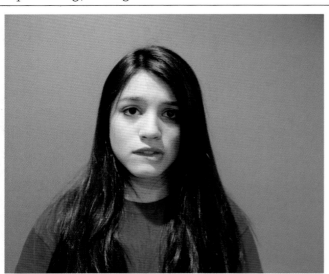

- In times of stress, blood and other fluids drain from our heads to our extremities.

- Pale faces and dry mouths are two signature fear and anxiety gesture cluster results.

- All of the senses are heightened, including pupil dilation, which causes light sensitivity, and a stronger sense of taste and smell.

- These defense mechanisms were adopted as a means of providing stronger fight-or-flight responses.

Anxious versus Natural Smile

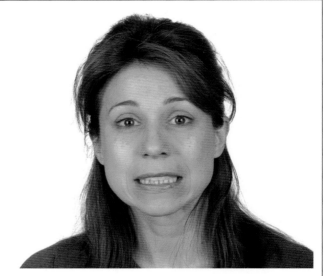

- In an anxious smile, the jaw is clenched, indicating discomfort and tension. The eyes appear wider than normal, which is a classic defense mechanism. Corners of the mouth will appear to pull slightly down and the mouth itself is only slightly open.

- In a natural smile, the jaw is relaxed, the eyes squint, the mouth is large and open, and the corners of the mouth pull up.

of messages to prepare a fight-or-flight response to the triggering situation. This results in, among other responses, an increase in heart rate and blood pressure, a tensing of muscles, a dilation of pupils, and a general heightening of senses. Our bodies are in preparation to fight off our stress-inducing culprit or flee from it. These nonverbal clusters of gestures are nonverbal communicators of fear and anxiety.

When these fight-or-flight responses coincide with other nonverbal indicators, such as leg or arm position, fear and anxiety can be denoted from the gesture clusters produced.

So, what are clusters anyway? It is important to understand that a gesture on its own can in fact provide but little context for what emotion the person is actually expressing. Imagine gestures as the words of our body's language. When individually examined, each gesture can draw any number of causes and conclusions. It is only when this gesture is given context (that is, presented alongside other gestures) that a conclusion can be drawn in regard to its meaning. Gestures can be most accurately deciphered when presented in clusters of three or more.

Ankles Crossed under Chair

- Locked ankles are a sign of restraint, whether this stems from needing to use the restroom or from withholding information.

- The gesture can signify that a person feels uncomfortable or edgy in the situation.

- "Keep your heels locked" is an old military expression that asks a person to not disclose all the available information.

- Avoid crossing your ankles if you'd like to project an image of confidence and honesty.

Rubbing a Palm across the Back of the Neck

- This can be a sign of frustration and anxiety that is often expressed by athletes and sports fans.

- When watching your favorite sports team, watch for an athlete's reaction to an unfavorable call. He might just remove his hat or helmet and rub the back of his neck.

- If still unsatisfied, he'll even throw his hat or helmet down onto the ground.

- Phrases that may derive from this action include "He gets in my hair!" and "She's a pain in the neck!"

DEFENSIVE
When words are not enough to protect us, our bodies step in

Let's return to the presentation you were giving. You survived the initial voice tremor and bad opening joke and have made it to the definitive portion of your speech. As your eyes scan the room, you notice your colleagues begin to cross their arms as they look at you. Did we forget to mention that your presentation topic was about a stricter policy enforcement in the workplace? To make yourself feel better, you grip the sides of your podium table, not noticing how white your knuckles now appear. The talk must go on, and so you power through the rest of this new and controversial policy update. The audience does not appear won over by your appeals, and before you know it your face goes red as you grow angry, and you snap out that you did not in fact write the policy; you were simply in charge of presenting it. When we feel threatened, we resort to defending ourselves, whether this involves a physical altercation or an emotional plea.

Crossing Arms

- This position covers the body's vital organs, a necessary defense in times of battle.

- Crossing arms is seen in professional peer-to-peer situations in which people might feel threatened by one another: Doctors around other doctors, teachers around other teachers, and so forth.

- This position is also commonly recalled as stance of a child defying his or her parent.

Grabbing the Back of a Chair

- This move creates a barrier between the two or more people involved in the situation.

- The chair creates additional space, a kind of safety zone for the person grabbing the chair.

- The person hides behind this chair from the other person.

- It is important to notice how tightly the person grips the chair to indicate level of defensiveness.

What you lacked was the ability to address the audience's negative attitude. Audience awareness is essential to persuasion. It is important to learn the art of recognizing what your audience is often silently screaming back at you. When you notice arms crossing as you talk with someone, this response is a shield from what you have to say, and the person is often withdrawn from the conversation. If he sits forward with his head tilted to the side, he may be interested in your topic of discussion. If his body is pointed toward the door halfway through your talk, it is probably best to take a short break, change your tone, or completely refocus your presentation because he is nonverbally communicating that he is ready for it to end.

Crossing Legs

- In negotiation situations crossing one's legs can signify doubt.

- It is difficult if not impossible to win a negotiation against someone with his legs crossed.

- People who cross their legs show that they are in competition and demand attention.

- If a person leans away and has his legs crossed, he is staying his ground in an argument or negotiation.

Attacking

- A person may lash out when he feels threatened.

- Animals also exhibit this behavior, dogs baring teeth and possibly biting before retreating.

- If attacked by a person in this manner, it is important to watch for other signs of defensiveness.

- Although this type of behavior denotes aggression and anger, if coupled with other defensive gestures, it is most likely part of a defensive gesture cluster.

EVALUATING

Processing information is the foundation of human thought and yet accompanies the least-recognized body language

We spend more time evaluating than any other form of behavior. Any time we think about, process, listen to, or watch something, we evaluate it. Imagine you are the teacher of a class of fifth-graders. As you begin your lecture for the morning, you see Charlie in the back of the class staring ahead at you with his feet planted on the ground and his posture straight. Upon initial glance, it appears that Charlie is paying attention to what you are saying. You, however, are not new to the field and are able to identify right away that Charlie is, in fact, zoning you out. He is simply doing a great job of hiding it. Next to Charlie is Ernie, sitting back in his chair, his hands folded across his chest. You know that he is definitely

Stroking of the Chin

- This gesture is often seen in the media as the classic form of thinking.

- It is exhibited cross-culturally.

- It can start as a gesture of the head resting in a hand.

- It is often seen in children as they watch parades or in people in the midst of a shared topic that interests them.

Tilting of the Head

- This is a sure sign of expressed interest.

- Animals show this behavior (often with forward raised ears) when they are interested.

- If a person is interested to hear more or did not catch the end of what you said, she will lean forward and tilt her head.

- The tilted head seemingly may be resting on the chin.

disagreeing with what you are presenting. Meanwhile, you look over at Holly, who is sitting forward in her chair with her eyes meeting yours and her slightly tilted head resting in her hand. She is paying attention and actively evaluating your lecture.

Understanding how others evaluate you will enable you to judge how well you convey information and how well the information you convey is received, whether people are actively engaged in what you are saying or you have turned them off to your point of view.

ZOOM

THE CRITICAL EVALUATOR: Her chin sits in the palm of her hand, her index finger extends up her cheek, and the rest of her fingers are curled and resting below her mouth. Her body is back or away from you, her legs may be crossed, and her other hand is potentially grasping the arm of her chair. Based on her gesture cluster, this woman is negatively, cynically, or critically evaluating you.

Looking Down and to the Left

- This is most likely exhibited during self-talk or thought.

- Most right-handed people will look to the left.

- This gesture is often seen in people recollecting memories.

- The position of the eyes is a field of study called "neurolinguistic programming" and will be discussed in Chapter 7.

A Bouncing Steeple

- A steeple is formed when two hands are placed together to resemble a position of prayer.

- The steeple, or person's hands, can be "bounced" forward and back in front of the chin or lips or on the desk.

- The more superior a person feels, the higher the steeple sits.

- This gesture can denote that a person knows more than he or she is saying.

CLUSTERING

35

SUBMISSIVE

We make ourselves look smaller to appear less threatening—and to win over our superiors

Remember when your worry list was comprised of which toy to ask for at the holidays or whether you could talk Mom into a lunch box consisting of a chocolate milk box and a couple of candy bars?

Now think back to when you got into trouble for exchanging your healthy homemade sandwich and apple for your best friend's extra candy bar. What did you do while Mom scolded you? Did you slouch over with your head tilted down? Was your foot rolling circles into the carpet? Were your hands either in front of you, one hand grabbing the wrist of the other, or tugging at your hair? When Mom threatened to take away your favorite game, did you beg with glossy

Chin Down, Eyes Averted

- This cluster will often also include the arms in front with one hand grabbing the other arm.

- In grabbing the arm, the person is shielding his vital organs.

- In lowering the head, the person is protecting the neck.

- Averting eyes is a sign of submission because the privilege of staring someone down is granted only to the dominant.

Eyes Big, Palms Up

- With the eyebrows up and the eyes wide open, a person mimics the vulnerability found in the faces of babies.

- Shrugging shoulders protects the neck and makes the person appear smaller.

- The hands extending forward with palms up are a classic sign of vulnerability.

- The extended hands with palms up show openness, sincerity, and agreement.

eyes looking up at hers? Did you throw your arms out to her, palms facing up, and swear to her that you would never, ever do it again? If so, you exhibited classic submissive gesture clusters that might have lessened your punishment. In showing Mom submission, you agreed to change your ways and submit to her demands, even if only to save yourself from losing that beloved game.

Not only children exhibit this type of behavior. Anyone hoping to win the respect of a superior may have to show vulnerability and acceptance of another's superiority. In the world of canines and felines, animals often demonstrate submission by lying on their back with neck and vitals organs exposed. In this position the dominant animal will most likely show mercy to the submissive animal and will not kill it.

Pulling, Playing with Hair

- This gesture denotes nervousness and makes a person appear younger.

- If it's not considered flirtation, the fidgeting behavior denotes insecurity and discomfort.

- This individual is likely to be submissive or lack confidence. This action is more or less the human version of the dog tucking its tail between its legs.

Becoming Small

- Slouching one's back and shoulders forward shows submission.

- Narrowing the stance shows how easily the person can be persuaded and guided.

- The hands in front show openness and a willingness to follow.

- In becoming small, the person shows that she is weaker than the opposing person.

POWER (HANDSHAKES)

The handshake greeting is one of the first opportunities we have to establish power

Whether you are meeting someone for the first time or reestablishing a connection, you probably have an idea of how you would like to be perceived—respectful, confident, powerful, and so forth. The handshake is often the initial contact between two acquaintances and can be varied to fit your specific goal.

For example, if your goal is to give power or respect to your acquaintance, you can appear more submissive by taking the lower position in the handshake and possibly averting eye contact. In addition, you have probably been taught that having a firm, dry handshake and maintaining eye contact during introductions or meetings are key to being perceived

Claim the Upper Hand

- When an individual shakes hands with his or her palm down toward the ground, it is a clear claim of dominance.

- This is where the expression "upper hand" comes from— the person with the palm facing down literally has the upper hand.

- This is a good move to assert power.

- The person with the lower hand is likely to feel your claim of superiority because this move is not very discreet.

Make a Hand Sandwich

- The hand hug, or hand sandwich, is another dominant handshake.

- Some give the hand hug automatically as an aggressive power play, others as a response to another's claim to the upper hand.

- If you are given the lower hand and want to regain some power, place your hand over your acquaintance's upper hand, grabbing the new upper hand for yourself.

- The sandwiching of your acquaintance's hand between yours gives you control.

as confident and equal. How does an ideal handshake change if you are trying to bypass both submissiveness and equality and instead assert dominance?

One way to set yourself up for a powerful handshake is to initiate the handshake itself. Walk confidently to the person you are meeting and extend your hand first. Eye contact is extremely important for a powerful handshake. When vying for power, make sure you get the top position in the handshake. You can also touch the upper arm of your acquaintance to further your control.

Grab the Upper Arm

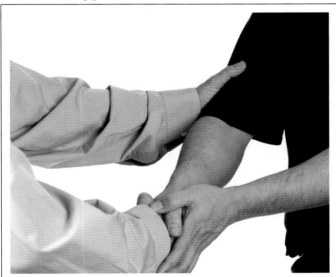

- The upper arm grab can be a friendly move but is extremely dominating when accompanied by other power moves.

- If you are given the hand hug, fight back by grabbing your acquaintance's upper arm—not too hard.

- By grabbing the upper arm, you reduce his or her mobility and gain back some power.

- The scenario described may sound excessive but is seen often between world leaders and other politicians.

Use Some Pull

- To further assert dominance, you may pull your acquaintance's hand into your personal space.

- By doing so you are taking the shake out of his personal zone, where he is likely to feel less comfortable.

- Pulling the handshake in toward you can also make the other person off balance.

- Because you are literally moving him, this move is very controlling and powerful—oftentimes too much so.

CLUSTERING

RELAXED (CONFIDENT)
The higher we hold our head and the less we touch our face, the more confident we appear

Why don't we just sit back and kick our feet up for a bit? Let's talk about confidence. Your father probably told you to stand up straight when you were a slouching kid and teenager and with good reason: People appear more self-assured, accomplished, and knowledgeable when they stand tall with squared shoulders. A confident person is less concerned with

his safety and will stand taller and not hide behind larger objects or people.

People who exude confidence and relaxation will touch their faces, play with their hair, or fidget with their hands or bodies much less frequently than people lacking in confidence. Confident people's heads will be held higher, and

Relaxed Body Posture

- Standing up straight reads as self-assurance.

- The wider a person's stance, the more dominant he appears to be.

- The less a person touches his face or fidgets, the more relaxed he is.

- Most people are drawn to a leader figure, and the more relaxed and secure a person appears, the more others will want to mimic and follow.

Use of Gestures

- Using gestures to illustrate your speech opens up your torso.

- Just as crossed arms make one appear closed off and shy, an open midsection makes one appear open and confident.

- Natural, purposeful gestures make the speaker appear competent, coordinated, and articulate.

- The use of confident gestures grabs the attention and interest of the audience, perpetuating the speaker's confidence.

their bodies will be more squared and open to others.

Confident and relaxed people tend to be leaders and stand dominant or superior in the workplace. The placement of one's feet can denote a position of power. When people place their feet on things, they show ownership. A confident and dominant person is more likely to have her toes stretched and pointed upward and legs kicked up onto furniture or desks. Watch out for subordinates exhibiting this kind of dominant behavior because it may lead to a power showdown.

The larger we appear, the more dominant and menacing we are perceived to be. Uncrossing our legs and opening our stance in a seated position show this dominance, as do raising our chest and widening a stance in a standing position. This "larger is dominant" concept has been extended to our possessions as well, from owning taller shoes to larger cars and bigger houses.

Showing Soles of the Feet

- This is a form of territorial rights assertion.

- Just as animals urinate and defecate to claim territory, people throw a leg over what they claim.

- The feet on the desk denote a level of power and confidence in a position of authority.

- This extends to pulling out a desk drawer and resting a foot on it.

Arm Draped over Chair

- This posture is used to show dominance or ownership even over the person in the chair.

- To exhibit this type of behavior, we might also spread our belongings over our own space or a space we are looking to claim.

- The hand draped over the chair will be open and unclenched in a relaxed manner.

- This gesture may be accompanied by sitting with legs open, exposing vulnerable areas of our body and taking up space, which shows dominance.

NEWBORN REFLEXES

Infants are born with a set of primitive reflexes that disappears within weeks

You might be asking yourself what babies and newborn reflexes have to do with a book about body language. The answer is this: Understanding how humans develop in the first years of life will shed light on the origins of communication. Do you realize, for example, that you were gesturing to express yourself before you learned to speak?

And even before you learned to gesture, you were born with about a dozen temporary primitive reflexes that reflect the biological evolution of humans. In our evolutionary past, these reflexes, or involuntary responses to stimuli, may have allowed helpless babies to survive in their precognitive states. For example, the Moro, or startle, reflex may have helped a baby cling to

Moro Reflex

- Here the legs and head extend while the arms jerk up and out with palms up and thumbs flexed. The baby looks as though he is embracing the air.

- This is known as the "Moro reflex," also called the "startle" or "embrace reflex," and disappears after three or four months of age.

- Stimuli include an abrupt repositioning of the head, a loud noise, or a temperature change.

- To test, with infant lying horizontal on his back, lift him slightly so his head drops back or make a loud noise.

Rooting Reflex

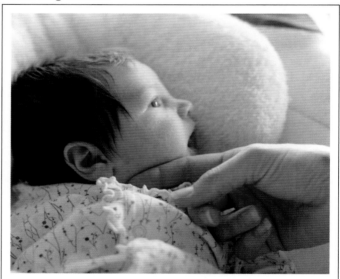

- Infants use their mouths to search for milk and move their heads in small arches to search for the source.

- This reflex assists in breast-feeding until four months of age, at which point the reflex becomes voluntary. This reflex may signal hunger.

- Stimuli include anything that brushes the cheek or mouth of the infant. Test with a gentle touch of the finger.

- Sucking is also a reflex that explains why babies will suck on anything placed into their mouth, including toys and fingertips.

his mother in case balance was lost. Today these reflexes don't serve much practical purpose in newborns, although they do signify healthy neurological development.

While reflexes are different from gestures and other body language signals, they are genetic precursors to nonverbal communication. The Moro reflex is closely tied to body language and can be triggered by exposing a baby to a loud noise. Though the reflex disappears in the early months of life, when we are caught by surprise or startled as adults, we still react almost involuntarily with a jump or a jerk.

Palmar Grasp

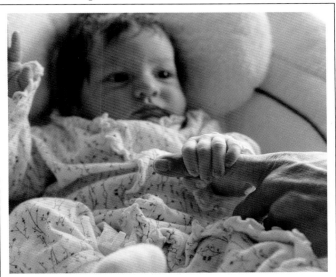

- Infants grasp and clutch any object that touches their palms.

- The infant's grip is almost strong enough to carry the baby's weight but can release at any point without warning. Pulling away from the infant will make the grip stronger.

- This may explain why babies are in the habit of clutching long hair and not letting go when they are picked up.

- The palmar grasp disappears after five to six months of age.

Stepping Reflex

- With foot soles touching a flat surface, a baby will initiate stepping by placing one foot before the other.

- Stimulus is a flat surface pressed against foot soles.

- To test, supporting the baby's weight under the arms as well as head, lean the baby slightly forward above the ground with soles on the floor.

- The stepping, or walking, reflex disappears after two to four months of age and reappears voluntarily between ten and fifteen months of age.

BABIES

43

HABITS
At four months babies develop signals to communicate and by nine months begin to gesture clearly

At around four weeks of age, a baby smiles for the first time—one of the most basic signals in body language. Between four and nine months of age, babies begin to physically communicate their basic needs, emotions, and reactions beyond crying and smiling. Of course, they still can't talk, so they rely on wiggling, waving limbs, and forming facial expressions.

Many of their movements seem universal among babies and can already be categorized into the kinesic groups discussed in Chapter 1. Signals being developed are based in cause and effect, such as raising the arms to be picked up. Although many of the motions, such as thumb sucking, are age-specific, other motions carry on into adulthood.

KNACK BODY LANGUAGE

Excited Affect Display

- An excited baby may smile or open his mouth, kick legs, wave arms, and breathe rapidly.

- This is an example of affect display that can appear in a baby under nine months of age.

- Another frequent emo-tional state is disgust, which displays on the face as squinting the eyes and pursing the lips and may include shaking the head.

- Of course, the most common affect display of all in babies is crying. See page 52 for information on how to understand crying.

Regulating Play

- A baby turning his head away may signify boredom, disinterest, or overstimulation.

- He may need a break from play or attention, or may want to change the activity.

- Regulators begin to be used as early as four months of age to control the flow of communication or stimulation.

- Turning the head away from a source of stimulation literally aids the brain in shutting out the stimulation because it becomes less perceptible to sight and hearing.

By nine months the cognitive growth of babies accelerates, and demonstrative gestures become coordinated. Babies might bang on the fridge for food or tug on their mother's clothes for attention. Expression of personal preferences advances, and a baby might hide or bury his face before strangers or greet family members with open arms.

Through the years opening the arms will continue to signify trust, openness, and friendliness, and hiding the body will continue to signal mistrust, fear, or close-mindedness. These basic principles of body language strengthen into adulthood.

Eye Rub

- A sleepy baby may rub his eyes, signaling it is time for a nap.

- This is a natural response to sleepiness even in adults and has a physiological purpose.

- Rubbing the eyes actually slows down our heart rate, consequently preparing us for sleep.

- If an adult engages in eye rubbing, it may indicate stress. Making this gesture physically assists in calming the body.

Ear Tug

- Babies tug, grab, pull, or scratch their ears for many reasons.

- Babies use this adaptor out of habit, especially when they want to comfort themselves.

- This gesture may also indicate sleepiness or an ear infection, or babies may do it when they are teething.

- In adults, pulling or tugging the ear may indicate indecision. Not all gestures retain their meaning into adulthood.

BABIES

45

SIGN LANGUAGE

Cut the crying: Infants can learn to communicate nonverbally at six months

Because we've established that babies grasp body language before they comprehend verbal language, doesn't it make sense that they should be able to use signing and gesturing as a tool to communicate?

The only prerequisite that a baby needs to learn sign language is to ensure that eye contact, or at least ten seconds of attention, can be maintained because this shows that the baby can focus on hand movement. After the baby has the cognitive skills to match a gesture to its object, then all that are needed are some motor skills to be able to make certain hand movements. After this is possible, the baby can communicate. It takes repetition and patience, but the baby will start to replace crying

Mommy

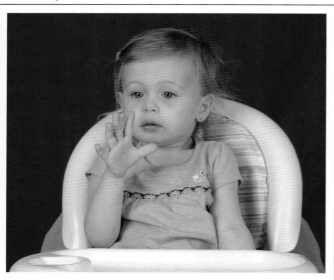

- To sign for "Mommy," spread fingers wide, touching the thumb to the chin.

- This can be simplified to just touching the chin if motor skills are still not refined.

- "Mommy" is one of the most important concepts in a baby's mind because she is depended on for survival.

- A baby needs to be able to sign for "Mommy" in order to identify her and call attention.

Daddy

- To sign for "Daddy," spread fingers wide, touching the thumb to the forehead.

- This can also be simplified to just touching the forehead if motor skills are not fully developed.

- Daddy is a protective figure in a baby's life as well as a guide and teacher.

- Being able to sign "Mommy" or "Daddy" brings much satisfaction not only to the baby but also to the parents.

with tangible expressions of needs and desires in the form of gestures such as those highlighted below. You can expect to start seeing results as early as six months of age and more advanced engagement by eight months of age.

Some parents might be skeptical. Won't this interfere with the baby's future development of speech? The answer is no, just the opposite. Research shows that signing early encourages language development in any form, including verbal. The kinesthetic elements reinforce verbal language as vocabulary is developed earlier, and future literacy will be improved.

Eat

- To sign for "eating" or "hunger," close the fingertips at or near the mouth.

- Simplify for baby by using just one finger at mouth.

- To teach this sign, show the baby food or a bottle and then clearly show the gesture.

- Guide the baby's hands to form the gesture before feeding.

Potty

- To sign for "potty," place the thumb between the index and middle fingers and shake the wrist several times.

- This may be a complicated gesture for a baby to make. It can be simplified in any manner.

- Being able to sign for "potty" will help avoid much discomfort and frustration.

- For prepotty-trained babies, the need for a diaper change can be expressed with this sign.

BABIES

CUTE FACTOR
We are predisposed to nurture and protect any living thing that possesses "cute" traits

Who would have ever thought that the survival of the fittest depends on being cute? Babies probably became cuter and cuter throughout their evolution. Just through body language and body image alone babies elicit in adults nurturing and protective attitudes.

This is why when we see a baby with small stature, chubby cheeks, big, wide eyes, inviting smile, button nose, and open arms most of us, especially women, instinctively feel heartwarmed or the desire to hug and protect the child. These cute traits are genetically and biologically purposeful. Biological anthropologists posit that "cuteness" attracted more attention and care from mothers, parents, caregivers, and

KNACK BODY LANGUAGE

Need for Nurture

- A baby needs to be nurtured and touched in order to develop emotionally and socially.

- A mother is naturally drawn to her "cute" baby and protects and keeps her child close.

- A cuddled baby is a healthy baby and is likely to progress positively. Baby massage is often used among parents to soothe babies. A common method is to subtly massage lotion back and forth on a baby's leg, almost like wringing out a wet towel.

Big Baby Eyes

- Big, wide, clear, expressive eyes make babies particularly pleasant to look at.

- Babies have a lot of pupil dilation, which is associated with positive mood.

- A baby's eyes are disproportionately larger than his head when compared with those of the average adult.

- The adorability of the alien ET from the hit movie may be due to his huge eyes, big head, and disproportionately small limbs that pull at our heartstrings. Big, cute baby eyes are marketable!

other adults, thus making babies more likely to survive.

Perhaps even more interesting is that when adults possess cute traits, they may be perceived as vulnerable or submissive, or they may be treated more compassionately. Women who make childlike faces, for example, are viewed this way. One example of making a childlike face is to tilt the head and chin down and to look up and out with the eyes. Princess Diana was in the habit of making this face and as a public figure was treated with great adoration and compassion by her fans.

· · · · · · · · · · · · · · · · · · · RED ● LIGHT · · · · · · · · · · · · · · ·

Do not adopt cute behavior or cute traits in a professional environment. This will likely not win you favor. If you are a naturally petite, or short-statured, person or possess a baby face, wear makeup that accentuates adult traits. If you are a male, pay extra attention to your attire by tucking in your shirt and polishing your shoes. You will gain more respect by highlighting your adulthood.

The Cute Voice

· Ever noticed that all babies have high-pitched, soft, and underdeveloped voices?

· As the jaw, lips, voice, tongue, and vocal cords develop, babies start with the soft vocalization of cooing, progress to babbling by six months, then start to try "nonsense speech" mimicking adult cadences.

· Adults tend to adopt the cutesy, high-pitched baby voice when communicating with babies.

· Tiny baby eardrums have a high resonant frequency, so they are relatively deaf to lower frequencies.

The Babyface Hypothesis

· A German research study on standards of beauty used the "babyface hypothesis" to underline popular notions of attractiveness.

· Ninety percent of test subjects found people (both men and women) with babyface traits and proportions more attractive than matured adult faces.

· Babyface attributes include big eyes, large, rounded forehead, and small nose and chin.

· Pouty lips, raised eyebrows, and lowered eyelids contribute to the effect.

BABIES

TODDLERS

Because their cognitive skills are still developing, toddlers depend on body language to express themselves

Toddlers do not hide their feelings. They are generally blaringly honest about what and whom they like or dislike and what their comfort levels are. Accordingly, their body language is overstated, blatantly expressed for all to see.

As body language evolves with social interaction and play, toddlers really begin to combine verbal and nonverbal language. Their negotiation of evolving communication skills is represented in several changes based in self-awareness.

As they develop a self-image and notions of self-control, they assert their bodies. Those foot-stomping tantrums, for example, are merely how toddlers cope with these transformations because they are not yet intellectually ready to

Terrible Twos

- Toddlers are renowned for their temper tantrums.

- Between the ages of two and seven, the prefrontal cortex of the brain in children is developing self-control.

- The tantrum is a coping mechanism. It is characterized by any of these signals: flushed and distorted face, screaming, banging arms, clenched fists, pulling of own hair, and rapid breathing.

- When dealing with a toddler's tantrum, remain calm and communicate with powerful gestures.

Monkey See, Monkey Do

- Toddlers are sponges. They observe and mirror people around them. Much of body language is learned by experience.

- Consequently, gestures, especially adaptors (habits and ticks), are passed down in the family.

- "Mirror neurons" are located in the Broca's area of the brain and are responsible for copying the actions of others.

- Imitation is vital to development and creates bonds with others.

discuss their issues logically. Toddlers also begin to experience self-conscious feelings, including embarrassment or shyness, which they show through averted gazes, hiding their face and clutching their mother.

The possessiveness that most toddlers display is related to an increasing sense of identity. Often their body language can be aggressive in nature. They may grab belongings from other children or assert their possessions—including Mom and toys—and accompany their actions with a strong verbal cue such as "Mine!"

It Wasn't Me!

- A guilty toddler may have a turned-down head, small, hunched shoulders, arms drooped in front, and legs close together.

- Toddlers are bad liars. Why? Lying with words is always obvious because body language is so pronounced.

- Toddlers are unable to control their revealing movements and lie at the same time.

- Other giveaways are expressing denial and smiling, avoiding gaze, hiding the face, hugging self, and squirming.

No!

- By stomping a foot, the toddler uses an illustrator to reinforce her verbal message, "No!"

- Saying and showing "No" is how toddlers assert themselves as they combine verbal and nonverbal skills.

- A common emblem for "No"

is tossing the head from side to side, which adults also do, only less dramatically. (Most toddlers exaggerate body language.)

- More extreme shows of negation or dislike are throwing self onto the floor or arching the back.

BABIES

DECIPHERING CRYING
Before crying turns hysterical, its distinct sound can be investigated for meaning

Babies cry in order to communicate. The problem with crying as communication is that it does not conceptualize wants and needs, and so parents have difficulty in specifying the issue at hand or remedying the problem.

Usually crying has to do with having hunger or potty needs, being fatigued, feeling too hot or cold, feeling overwhelmed, desiring to be held, or feeling aches and pains. Pay close attention to reflexes such as rooting or Moro. These can indicate that an infant under four months of age is hungry or startled. If the baby is over six months of age, look for body language cues, such as banging on the table, shaking fists, or rolling the head, that accompany the crying.

Hungry

- A baby is likely to become hungry when he sees food.

- After the food is spotted and hunger ensues, the baby will turn and possibly reach toward the food and emit a low cry or moan.

- The cry will become more urgent as he focuses on his desire to eat.

- One study shows that when the sucking reflex of newborns is triggered by hunger, it impacts the sound of the cry, causing a recognizable "neh" sound.

Sleepy

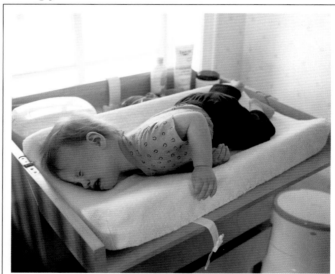

- A sleepy baby will usually express fatigue through whining or moaning.

- The baby will not necessarily shed tears.

- The sleepy whine is commonly heard right before nap time and is accompanied by being cranky, rubbing the eyes, and yawning.

- In newborns the yawn reflex is triggered and may cause the cry to sound like "owh," which is long and pronounced.

Paralanguage is the nonverbal elements of communication (pitch, volume, and intonation of speech or vocally produced sound). To decipher crying, look to the expressive aspects of paralanguage that affect loudness, pitch, range, and rate. It can point to intentional and unintentional feelings and distinguish faked or exaggerated emotions.

Crying can be moaning, whining, yelling, or high-pitched screaming. Body reactions that accompany crying are squirming, shaking, flushing, gasping, and shedding tears.

Pain

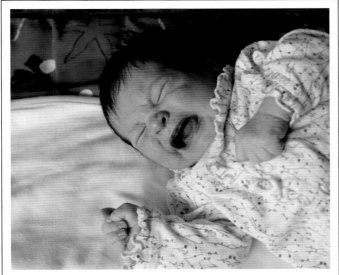

- If a baby suddenly starts to scream without any previous build-up of crying, this can be a sign of pain.

- The scream will be high pitched and may be accompanied by wailing and gasping.

- The pain may result from a fall or a bump or from a shocking and unexpected event.

- The pain can even be emotional, such as a reaction to the mother going away or leaving the room.

Discomfort

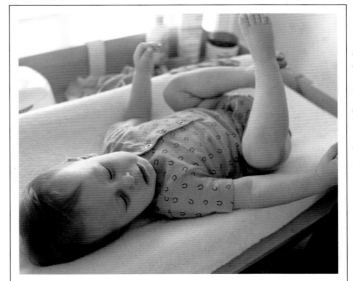

- Discomfort is expressed by a fussy crying.

- The baby will squirm and cry simultaneously and become increasingly frustrated.

- The reasons for discomfort can be many. Baby sign language would really help in this uncomfortable situation.

- A newborn may emit a repeated "heh" sound in his cry, indicating he may want to be in a new position or needs a diaper change.

BABIES

WOMEN'S MOVES

Body language is second nature to alpha leaders, who use it abundantly and possess a keen eye for others' moves

Women have ways of moving and gesturing that distinguish them from men. For example, they take up less space, tend not to be expansive with their movements, and typically show more emotional expression on their faces, especially when it comes to smiling and crying. You generally won't see a woman sitting with her legs wide apart in a crotch display stance and both her arms spread out behind her on a sofa or bench as some men do. Look around on a subway or bus stop at how women carry themselves.

Women are also known to show more affect display. In a male-female couple, who is more likely to shed tears during a sappy film? You don't have to be Sherlock Holmes to figure

Looking When Talking

- Why does a mother say to her child, "Look at me when I'm talking to you!"? It's because she uses eye contact to infer the truth.

- Years of research show women tend to make more eye contact than men in conversation because they

are often more socially oriented and interested in bonding.

- One study of two-to four-day-old newborn girls shows them maintaining twice as much eye contact with adults as do boys.

Tucking in the Body

- Many intraverted or shy beta leaders tend to "tuck in" their bodies to take up less space or appear smaller, especially in public.

- She will tuck her feet under her chair, perhaps with crossed legs or ankles, and she may keep her arms close. Her purse is usually

clutched closely to her.

- This submissive body language is self-protecting or defensive in nature.

- Remember that it doesn't necessarily mean the woman is submissive because it may just happen to be a habitually feminine trait.

out it's probably not the man. Generally woman are more aware of their bodies and the signals they send.

You can imagine that the stereotype for women's body language as femininity is defined by gentler, more graceful moves, generally smaller than and not as aggressive as men's. Some may call women's moves "submissive." However, thanks to the sexually alpha female movement these days, women defy that stereotype. They are actually quite assertive with their gestures, eye contact, and posture, making them effective communicators.

The Feminine Handhold

- Despite several studies claiming that woman use their nondominent hand when holding hands with men, my research indicates hand-holding positions are situational.

- Although there does tend to be some truth to the claims that women tend to face their palm forward, this may be due to the fact that men are taller.

- This is regarded as a submissive move because the man's hand leads the way, guiding not only the woman's hand but also her entire body in his intended direction.

Woman Courting

- Although many women engage in moves that hide or minimize their bodies, courtship can elicit just the opposite in a female.

- Women who want to attract a love interest may display their bodies through exaggerated juxtaposing of body parts highlighting feminine traits.

- With the bust jutting forward, the lower back curved to enhance the bottom, a tilted hip, and a form of self-touch, such as a finger on the neck or lips, a woman is sending a very strong sexual signal.

MEN'S MOVES

Alpha males make big moves and fill up space because they tend to favor displays of power and status

Alphas have a natural propensity to "take up more room," filling the space around them with their stance and gestures and making use of objects near them. They have a greater tendency than betas to lean on walls or tables, to sit with their legs and arms widely stretched apart, or stand with ample width between their feet—what is called "open posture."

Again, you must consider these basic traits as generalizations. They simply indicate masculine habits but do not define masculinity per se. Taking up space and using broad body language are natural ways of expressing authority, power, and confidence. If a man is leaning on a wall or comfortably taking over the entire sofa, he is showing proximal

The Lounge

- An alpha sitting with widely stretched, open limbs, lounging, and extending his body over furniture is displaying a classic male pose.

- By making himself comfortable in the environment, he conveys confidence and dominance.

- His body language defines and possesses the space.

- His body language embodies the expression "king of the castle."

Figure-4 Leg Cross

- Whereas betas are more likely to cross their legs at the knees, men usually sit with one leg propped over the other.

- This posture creates the figure 4 and is a much more open stance than knee crossing, exposing the legs and bottom of foot.

- It also displays the crotch area, a sign of virility.

- Betas who sit like this are usually in a very laidback environment.

ownership over those areas and probably feels quite cool and confident, certainly self-assured. At worst he might just be arrogant as his body conveys, "I am king of the castle."

So far we have made the typical body language of males seem pretty ego driven. Whether they know it or not, men unconsciously move to assert power, control, authority, and dominance. An aspect besides ego that plays a large role in how men move is the primitive urge to defend as well as to hunt.

ZOOM

Alpha men engage in "nonreciprocal touching" or touching without being touched back. Often it is a form of "patriarchical" touching. Look at family portraits, especially old ones and you will see the father figure with a hand on his wife's and children's shoulders. Men should practice caution in touching women; it can often be perceived as harassment as it is unsolicited intimacy.

Crotch Communication

- It is common to see men standing and covering their "valuables" with their hands when in public or before a crowd.

- Because the man is hiding a vulnerable area, he is protecting himself.

- The gesture indicates that he needs to feel secure. For example, if he is in front of an audience, he may not want to feel exposed.

- This gesture is exclusive to men for obvious reasons.

The Cowboy

- A cowboy is a classic figure of macho manliness.

- In the cowboy stance an alpha stands with his hands in his pockets and thumbs pointing in the direction of his front zipper. His legs and feet are set widely apart.

- This is the classic stance of male virility and is a sign of courtship.

- A man will assume this pose in front of a woman he wants to attract as if to state his exact intentions.

WOMEN VERSUS MEN

Who's the expert? Let's take a look as the sexes approach body language

Is it true that women have a sixth sense? If you count the ability to read body language as a sense, then maybe so. Women generally show more aptitude in communicating nonverbally than men and seem to be adept at understanding people.

A Harvard study calculated that women read a social situation accurately 87 percent of the time, whereas men do only 42 percent of the time. Men in nurturing professions (such as nurses) and artistic professions and gay men did nearly as well as women.

One explanation is motherhood. As mothers rear children, they must be able to communicate with them nonverbally in the early years. Whatever the reason, science shows that

Nonverbal Mothering

- The nonverbal skills a mother gains through childrearing and an inborn female ability to decipher body language are applied in daily communication throughout a lifetime.

- Interestingly, mothers produce milk at the sound of a baby's cry.

- Mothers are physiologically and mentally equipped to utilize body language.

- For example, during a game of peek-a-boo, the mother is communicating with gestures and eye contact while also introducing a verbal cue to her baby.

Male Mistakes

- Guys: Don't assume that a woman's friendliness indicates flirtatious attraction.

- All too often inexperienced men misinterpret women's body language, giving it the benefit of the doubt.

- Just because she's smiling doesn't mean she's inter-

ested! Look for a cluster or other signals to figure out true feelings.

- Look for courtship signals discussed previously if she's interested or look for signs, such as turning the face or body away, indicating nonromantic intent.

women's brains actually possess more neural capacity for communication than men's. They are literally hardwired to be potentially excellent communicators. In fact, studies show that from the outset of life, baby girls show more interest in communicating than do baby boys.

But where does this leave men? Don't get too confident, ladies, because men's brains are better at seeing patterns and abstract relationships. Apply this to body language, and they may be quite skillful at exposing less obvious or nonvisible factors and complex elements.

YELLOW LIGHT

Why are men often confused by women and blame them for being indirect, whereas women accuse men of not listening? Part of this problem may be biological because women have five vocal tones, and men are able to pick up on only three of them, risking a loss of communication.

Self-monitoring

- When a man looks at a woman and she is aware of it, she may be very conscious of her body signals and is able to view herself from the onlooker's perspective.

- John Berger, author of *Ways of Seeing*, points out that female models in advertisements will look at the camera as if it were a male onlooker.

- Given these facts, women have a keen awareness of their body language and how it is received.

Vision

- Men tend to have tunnel vision, whereas women have greater peripheral vision.

- Though men have greater target ability, they might not see the whole picture as women do.

- Because men are programmed for hunting, they have a narrow field of vision, which gives them a good sense of direction.

- After a face-to-face conversation, a woman may be more likely than a man to recall what a person looked like head to toe.

FACE OFF

Basic facial expressions are universal, but men and women don't always use them the same way

Men and women tend to differ when it comes to how much expression they display on their faces. Men are known to have a monotonic facial expression more often than women, paralleling their stereotypical tendency to bottle or hide their internal feelings. Conversely, women are known to have highly expressive faces, showing emotion on them frequently.

The discrepancy often causes issues between men and women. Consider the following: Man masks emotions on his face; woman mistakes the neutrality for negative feedback. Anxiety or confusion ensues. But it's not just the man causing the breakdown in communication. How many times have you heard it said that women "overanalyze"?

KNACK BODY LANGUAGE

Straight Face

- Some men tend to show emotion on their faces less frequently.

- As a result, their faces can seem monotonic or statuesque, and others may assume that there is an absence of emotion.

- Women may read this lack of display on the face negatively. Loss of communication can ensue.

- Men who have trouble with facial expressions can try mirroring others' expressions in order to be better understood.

Anger Associated with Men

- Expressions of anger, including tight lips and lowered brow, are usually associated with men.

- An experiment by the University of Quebec in Montreal, androgynous faces with angry expressions were shown to both sexes. These were more likely to

- be identified as male.

- Expression of anger is used to protect, defend, or threaten and is considered dominant in nature. A man's naturally louder, deeper voice can make his vocal expression of anger seem much more intimidating than a soft, feminine voice.

Despite men's commonly limited use of facial expressions, one study actually shows that men are more adept than women at spotting anger. In a joint study by Dr. Williams from the Massachusetts Institute of Technology and Jason B. Mattingley from the University of Melbourne in Australia, men were faster than women at picking out angry faces. Anger was also more easily spotted in male faces than female faces. This ability in men is a primitive response to threat or danger. However, in picking out happy, sad, surprised, or disgusted faces, women were still faster than men.

On the opposite end from anger is smiling, usually an expression of joy (though not always). Smiling happens to be more prevalent in women and is used by women to strengthen social bonds and encourage children. However, in some cultures and contexts smiling is the same among both sexes. Caucasian females in the United States may smile more frequently than men, but among African Americans, men and women smile at the same rate. Furthermore, women and men habitually smile when under observation, and both tend to smile the same in professional environments.

Happiness Associated with Women

- In the same Canadian study that showed anger associated with male faces, happy faces were usually identified as female or feminine.

- Smiling occurs more frequently in women than in men—an inborn trait.

- Smiling is considered both nurturing and submissive.

- Fear is also a facial expression that is more closely associated with women.

The Face of Innocence

- Some women tilt their heads down and point their eyes up when looking.

- Teamed with any expression, the face becomes childish because this is a common gesture of children.

- This can turn any expression into innocence. It invokes compassion and protection from those who see it.

- The gesture makes any expression appear not only more childish but also more feminine.

GENDER ROLES
How to use masculinity and femininity as a male or female

In the days of old, men were men and women were women . . . so they say. Look at any Victorian (turn of the twentieth century) family portrait, and you will notice how the paternal head of the family embodies masculinity, and the maternal role embodies femininity both in dress and stance. We generally think of the Victorians (you know, Jane Austen, tea parties, social reputations, chastity) as having strict gender roles. In some ways they did and often took them too far.

Did you know that many Victorian women dressed their male children in female attire? (Dresses, ribbons, pink, lace—the works!) Yes, America's manliest literary genius, Ernest Hemingway, was actually dressed as a girl when he was a child. That's a fact.

Today we are more lenient with interchanging masculine and feminine traits among the sexes. Often it is beneficial to adopt particularly feminine or masculine body language in

Women Try on Masculinity

- In decades past women mostly stayed home with the kids and took a submissive role in both the household and society.

- In a male-dominated environment, women can tone down feminine dress and body language for credibility.

- Businesswomen today dress in professional suits, use firm handshakes, maintain direct eye contact, and so forth to establish gender equality.

- Women with too much masculine body language, when overdone, are often perceived as bossy or negatively controlling.

Men Try on Femininity

- Over the course of history, men have been seen as the dominant gender.

- In newly female-dominated environments, men may want to tone down masculine body language to ensure smooth communication/ nonaggression.

- Men who take on some traditionally female occupations such as nurses, designers, and homemakers, can do so today without the fear of being judged.

- Men with too much feminine body language are often perceived as weak and have less credibility.

certain situations. For example, for a woman in a professional setting, downplaying female traits and feminine submissiveness is best for success and credibility in the workplace.

But even what is considered feminine and what is considered masculine are starting to become unclear, and they begin to overlap. Today stay-at-home dads are considered as manly as ever, and just because a man acts submissive does not mean he has a poorly developed Y chromosome.

RED ● LIGHT

In recent years as more women have entered the workforce, we see that the traditional gender based body language is becoming less and less relevant. Very soon this notion may be better described by alpha and beta body language types.

Body Awareness

- One study has shown when passing other men turn toward the other person 75 percent of the time, while women turn toward only 17 percent of the time.

- This could be because women are usually more protective of their body

- when not looking to establish an intimate relationship.

- Men do not think of having to ward off unwanted attention and therefore are less aware of their bodies in an everyday setting.

Changing Roles, Changing Moves

- As men and women adopt roles that were once unacceptable in society, such as a female politician and a male nurse, body language norms change.

- Women have started to adopt more assertive body language.

- Whereas once their moves had to be graceful, soft, and submissive, today's world requires their body language to be much more powerful and dominant.

- Similarly, the body language and body habits of men change with time as it becomes socially acceptable for men to be less apparently dominant and typically manly.

63

GENDER IN HISTORY

Look at some of the habits of the sexes and how they've evolved through history

We've already touched upon history by discussing the Victorians and their adherence to traditional notions of masculinity and femininity. That is only one example of gender roles in history. Actually, until around the turn of the twentieth century, roles stayed rigidly the same, and male and female duties barely evolved. Only in the twentieth century was

there a real move to change these conventions, and it mostly changed only for women. Men are only starting to assume new roles and pick up new body language.

Through most of time, men and women had small habits, traditions, and body language styles specific to their gender—we can only wonder at the origin of them today.

Buttons and Buckles

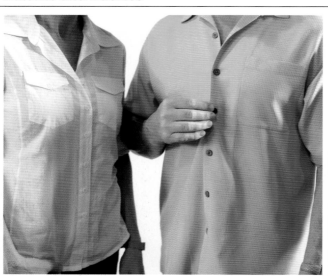

- Ever wonder why men's and women's buttons and buckles attach on opposite sides?

- Men's buttons used to be on the left, whereas women's were on the right. (Now the opposite is true.)

- One theory is that men had to be able to pull their weapons out of their garments quickly (assuming they were right-handed).

- Another theory posits that women were buttoned by their maids (most people are right-handed), so buttons were inverted for the sake of the dresser.

Bendy Wrist

- In olden times women were severely restricted by their clothing.

- Stiff, tight corsets as well as skirt frames and layers of fabrics made it difficult for women to move their joints and limbs with ease.

- Women in these times habitually bent their wrists to extreme degrees and expressed much through those agile wrists.

- The theory is that because the wrists were freer to move than the other clothed body parts, they were used more often.

For example, why do men and women have buttons on opposite sides? Why is the wrist—and in particular a floppy, bendable wrist—considered feminine? What sociological developments in history happened to determine what was feminine and what was masculine? Many of these nuances derive from old traditions that are lost to us today. Sociologists offer an abundance of theories to answer these questions. Let's take a look at a few of them in the images below.

ZOOM

After studying the first image on the previous page about button placement history, think of your own theories. Did women's buttons switch sides (to the left) in order that women could be on equal footing with men at the turn of the century when the switch occurred?

Anatomical Advantage

- Though this is more scientific than historic, women's ability to rotate their forearm to extreme degrees plays a role in sociology.

- The evolutionary advantage of this ability is that women can carry their children.

- With the nuances that came about through society and history, it became an attractive feature, not just practical.

- Thus, forearm rotation is highly feminine and attractive to men.

Art and Body Language

- A great way to study body language through history is to observe paintings and sculptures.

- In baroque sculptures, you can see that men's and women's bodies are dramatized, and stance and posture are full of movement and rhythm.

- In sculptures and paintings from the Middle Ages, you notice much more rigid and stiff bodies as well as austere facial expressions.

- By studying the body language of men and women in portraits, you have a key to understanding their roles in history.

PUPIL GIVEAWAYS
Eyes are actual "windows to the brain," and it's all in the pupils

Although the pupil's main function in the human eye is to regulate the absorption of light so that we can see well both in dark and bright environments, it also serves as a literal "window to the brain." As you may know, pupils dilate and expand in dark conditions and constrict and shrink in bright conditions. What you may not have learned in biology class is that pupillary reactions can also be the result of psychological effects. And because it is an unconscious occurrence that

we cannot control, pupil size is often a tell-tale sign about how we feel or how we process information.

Biopsychologist Eckhard Hess coined the term *pupillometry* in 1975. His research showed that pupils dilate in response to positive stimuli such as being sexually aroused or solving a problem and contract when viewing or feeling negative, boring, or unpleasant things. We also subconsciously notice pupil size in others, affecting our attitudes toward them.

The Constricted Pupil

- This young woman has small, constricted pupils.

- Either this is a physiological reaction to bright light, or she may be observing something that she dislikes.

- You may find that her small pupils affect your opinion of her appearance. It would

be a natural response to perceive her as less interesting, friendly, or attractive here than in the following photo, in which her pupils are dilated.

- Pupils also contract just before someone falls asleep.

The Dilated Pupil

- You may find this woman to seem friendlier, more approachable, and more attractive than in the image to your left.

- This is probably because her pupils are dilated, making her eyes seem large, warm, and inviting.

- We are naturally more drawn to dilated pupils.

- In the sixteenth century the belladonna ("beautiful woman" in Italian) plant was made into a tincture and dropped into the eyes by women in order to enlarge pupils.

A pupillometer is a device that measures the diameter of pupils. It is mostly used by medical personnel or by law enforcement personnel to determine when someone is under the influence of narcotics. It also is used by authorities to detect deception. Without a pupillometer, all you need is good vision, and you should be able to spot pupil sizes up to 6 feet away.

EYES

Eliciting the Dilation

- Pupil dilation is caused by positive stimuli and a positive reaction in the brain.

- What causes dilation differs from person to person, based on gender, culture, and personal preferences.

- Men's pupils almost always dilate when they see someone they are attracted to.

- Women's pupils also dilate when they are aroused. They have a strong pupil dilation reaction when they see babies and children.

Mirrored Pupils

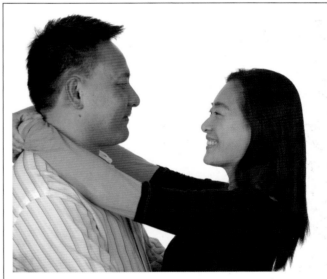

- Pupils dilate not only in response to outer and inner stimuli but also in response to others' pupils.

- People's pupils will mirror each other. That is, if you gaze into the eyes of someone with dilated pupils, yours will automatically enlarge.

- The same goes for constricted pupils.

- Pupil dilation and constriction are out of our hands. They are an unconscious occurrence, and we cannot control them unless lighting is manipulated.

GAZING FACE-TO-FACE

Be aware of how you gaze at another person during conversation and what message it sends

Whereas a glance is a short look, and a stare is a long look, a gaze is an intent and steady look that varies in meaning depending on several factors. When engaging with a person, especially in conversation, gazing usually involves directing your eyes to someone's face. But you can also gaze at other body parts or even objects. Gazing signifies that something

has our attention. The question to ask when understanding what kind of attention a gaze holds is, "Where is its focus?" Observe the line of vision. The gaze can be focused directly in the eyes; it can be directed at just the forehead or the lips; or it can be defocused, looking at the entirety of a person's body. A gaze can also move up and down or even avoid the

The Standard Gaze

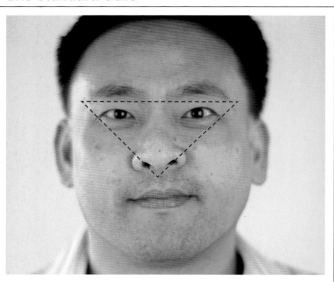

- When conversing with someone, you usually gaze into an upside-down triangular area between the eyes and mouth on the person's face.

- Direct, unbroken eye contact is not the norm and is not considered standard for social encounters.

- Gazing on this area of the face makes others perceive you as nonaggressive.

- Staring at one spot on someone's face will make the person uncomfortable. She may think there is a blemish or food on her face.

The Impact Gaze

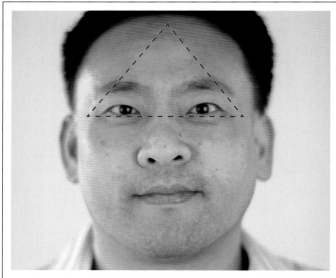

- A right-side-up triangular area from the middle of the forehead to the eyes is a powerful gaze focus.

- It impacts the person being gazed at by making him feel your authority.

- He will feel pressure as your gaze pins him down.

- To maintain this kind of effect, do not drop your eyes below his. The impact gaze can be used to intimidate or impose.

other person by being aimed at the floor or beyond the person's shoulder.

Take a man who gazes at a woman's lips either intermittently or steadily during a conversation. If you know that lips convey sensuality (this is why women wear lipstick), then you might guess that a gaze directed at the lips more than once and more than briefly can be a sign that the gazer may be interested in more than the words coming out of her mouth. He may want a kiss, subconsciously or not.

The Attraction Gaze

- The lips, chest, and groin are all associated with sensuality or sexuality.

- When looking someone in the eye, if your gaze strays down to any or all of these areas individually, it is likely that you find the person attractive.

- Although many people may not pay attention to what part of their own face is being gazed at, they will be aware of a gaze directed at the chest or groin.

- The attraction gaze can be done unconsciously, so be careful if you want to be discreet about your feelings.

The Sizing-up Gaze

- If your gaze travels vertically over a person's whole body, you may be sizing him up.

- That is, you are taking in his overall presence, his dress, posture, and mannerisms.

- Your observations are catalogued in your mind whether you realize it or not.

- Imagine two boxers in a ring. They look each other up and down in order to be familiar with their competitor before beginning the round.

EYE CONTACT

Looking people in the eye is a form of attention and acknowledgment that reveals sincerity

We humans tend to look at each other in the eyes when we communicate. It is part of social bonding. In conversation eye contact indicates that we have each other's attention. This mutual awareness creates trust and honesty, strengthening alliances and relationships. Why, for example, in our culture is it so important to look at a newly met person in the eyes during a handshake? It has to do with recognition and establishes the groundwork for future communication. Eye contact can also be "accessorized" by blinking, and close attention should always be paid to blinking rate or absence of blinking.

When eye contact is avoided, it can lead to mistrust. Avoiding eye contact is often seen as a basic sign of deception. A

Avoiding Eye Contact

- When someone is speaking and their eye contact is limited, it could be an alarm for dishonesty because averting eye contact is a form of concealment. It may also signify shame or guilt.

- However, a practiced liar knows not to hide the eyes.

- Caution: Auditory people are naturally less focused on eye contact and tend to "lend you an ear."

- A person may also avoid eye contact if he is shy or insecure or is experiencing social anxiety.

The Nonblinking Eyes

- Be careful. Consistent eye contact with no blinking can indicate dishonesty because an experienced liar purposefully maintains eye contact to avoid suspicion.

- Liar giveaway: The blinking is forcibly restricted, smiling is done with the mouth and not the eyes, and the overall gaze may seem too intense and a bit off.

- No blinking could also mean that a threat is being "stared down."

- Persistent and prolonged eye contact can be intimidating.

70

liar naturally wants to hide his lying eyes. Experienced liars are aware of this and may tactically do just the opposite by staring intently to cover this up.

Too much or prolonged eye contact, such as staring, can be perceived as threatening, aggressive, or rude. Many animals see direct eye contact as a threat. One of the most pervasive traits in children with autism is avoidance of eye contact. Brain research conducted at the University of Wisconsin–Madison shows that autistic children perceive even the gazes of familiar faces as threats.

Gaze Aversion

- Anyone engaged in concentration may avert the gaze and break eye contact in order to better process information.

- Social eye contact can be distracting. When "all eyes are on you," you may lose your train of thought.

- A University of Sterling study found this to be true among young students when doing calculations.

- When making eye contact, your brain is involved in a form of attentive visual communication. It is hard to look someone in the eye and do math at the same time.

EYES

MAKE IT EASY

How long should you maintain eye contact before it is considered staring? People usually look at each other in the eyes between one and seven seconds and then look away. Intermittent glancing is the norm during a conversation, and the listener will look at the speaker more than the speaker looks at the listener.

Eye Contact for Shy People 101

- Concentrate on one eye. Don't dart from eye to eye when you are looking at someone.

- Avoid staring and don't forget to blink. When you are nervous, it shows in your eyes. Strive for a relaxed gaze.

- If you are nervous about eye contact, truly listening to what the other person has to say will take your mind off of your anxiety. Your eye contact will become natural without your having to try.

- Staring into the eyebrows gives the illusion of eye contact.

EYES & THOUGHT
Look at where the eyes are pointed to learn how a person is thinking

By observing eye directions, you can almost mind read because these positional glances or gazes are direct reflections of brain activity. Before studying the images below and on the following pages to understand what looking up, down, left, or right specifically means, you must first connect these directions to the two halves of the brain. The right

hemisphere of the brain processes emotion, whereas the left processes logic. The brain correspondences switch sides in the body, so when a right-handed individual looks to the right, his left brain is activated, and his thoughts probably have a logical basis. When he looks to the left, his right brain is activated, and his thoughts are emotional. Sometimes the

Up and Right

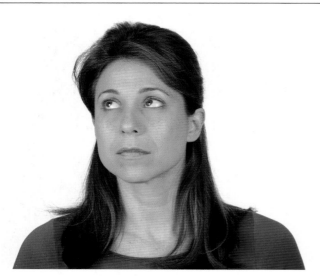

- Looking up is visualization, whereas looking right is imagining.

- Together these mean that an image is being created and constructed in the mind's eye.

- For example, answer the question, "What would a polka-dot chicken look like?"

- The imaginative and emotional right brain tries to conceive the answer by constructing a creative image.

Right

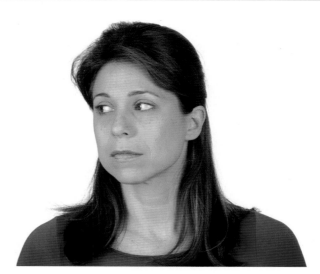

- Eyes looking sideways have to do with sound, whereas eyes looking right have to do with imagining.

- A sound is being constructed in the brain.

- For example, answer the question, "What does rain on a tin roof sound like?"

- Again, the right brain takes on the creative task of imagining such a sound.

opposite is true for left-handed individuals, though this is not always the case, and they are less predictable. (The images below are more typical for righties.)

NLP, or neurolinguistic programming, is the science behind eye direction. NLP encompasses the dynamics between mind and language, which interplay with body and behavior. According to NLP eye accessing cues, looking right signifies imagining, whereas looking left is remembering. Looking up is a visual thought, whereas looking to the sides toward the ears indicates thought that has to do with sound. Looking down and right is recalling emotions, whereas looking down and left is internal dialogue.

To apply these rules, consider this theoretical situation: You are explaining all this to a friend. While pausing to grasp the concepts of NLP, your friend looks up. By his looking up, you know it is clear that his brain is trying to visualize what is being learned. Instead of trying to explain with more words, try demonstrating or showing the images below in order to satisfy his visual needs.

Down and Right

- Looking down is kinesthetic thought, or self-perception, whereas looking right is imagining.

- A feeling or emotion is either being explored or constructed as a hypothetical circumstance.

- Answer the question, "How would you feel if you were dumped and won the lottery on the same day?"

- It can also indicate recalling past emotions, which are reimagined or refelt.

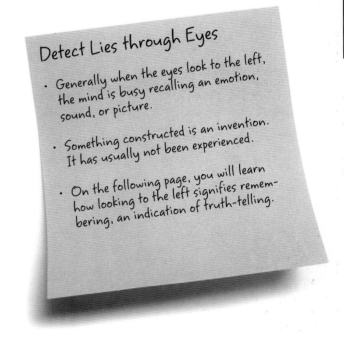

Detect Lies through Eyes

- Generally when the eyes look to the left, the mind is busy recalling an emotion, sound, or picture.

- Something constructed is an invention. It has usually not been experienced.

- On the following page, you will learn how looking to the left signifies remembering, an indication of truth-telling.

73

EYES & THOUGHT (CONT.)

Eye-accessing cues are not absolutes; you can baseline a person's gaze direction tendencies

Eye directions and their corresponding thoughts are certainly not set in stone. The NLP eye-accessing cues are not absolute indicators of types of thought and just reflect the most common patterns. Individuals vary and not only because they are lefties or righties or dominated by the left or right brain. Individuals just happen to have habits that are unique to themselves. This is where calibrating and baselining become important. You must be able to map out those habits in order to figure out how the rules apply to them. Who knows? A person could just have a personal tendency to look up and right when considering an emotion. A good observer of body language notices these divergences.

Up and Left

- Looking up is visualization, whereas looking to the left is remembering.

- Together these constitute recalling an image or a visual memory.

- Answer the question, "What did your grandmother look like?"

- Your left, logical brain reaches into the files of your memory to come up with the answer.

Left

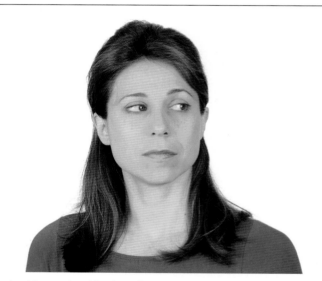

- Looking to the sides is auditory thought, and looking to the left is remembering.

- This eye direction signifies that a sound, voice, or music is being recollected.

- Answer the question, "What was the last song you heard on the radio?"

Critics of the visual accessing cues deny any existence of the pattern and consider it hocus-pocus. However, test out conversing with several people and note their eye directions. You will be surprised how many fit the pattern. However, as mentioned, do not accept these rules as absolutes, especially if you need to determine whether someone is lying. You usually won't have just one giveaway. Lying is complex, and tracing a lie through body language is a complicated process involving many more factors than just one eye movement.

ZOOM

If a person tends to look in a certain direction (up, down, or sideways) more often than the others, it may mean that he is drawn to a type of thinking. He may have what is called a "preferred representational system" as an auditory, kinesthetic, or visual thinker (and learner). If you can establish her habitual preference, you can communicate with her on the same bandwidth.

Down and Left

- Looking down reflects kinesthetic thought or self-perception, whereas looking to the left reflects a logical or verbal process of the left brain.

- The down and right direction indicates an internal monologue (self-talk).

- People talk to themselves in their heads while they are not interacting with others.

- They also engage in self-talk while making judgments about those they are talking to, that is, "This guy's a know-it-all. Good thing he can't read my mind!"

Eye-accessing Cues Quiz

- Test yourself. Can you figure out the eye directions for the following thoughts?

- What would jazz music sound like under water? Hint: sound constructed.

- My stomach is hurting, and I feel anxiety about this discomfort. Hint: self-talk that is kinesthetic or having to do with physical or emotional feelings.

- My car is a blue minivan. Hint: visually remembering.

EYEBROWS

The second most expressive feature on the face—your eyebrows—may be saying more than you think

Eyebrows are not only accessories to the eyes. The angles at which brows are bent or raised can change the entire aspect of a facial expression and magnify the subtler signals of the eyes.

Without eyebrows our faces lose a valuable expressive tool. It is much harder to read a face without eyebrows. As expressive entities in and of themselves, the brows have a remarkably wide range of emotional signals. Look in the mirror and maintain a still, expressionless face. Then move only your brows. See how many different expressions you can create with them alone. Anger, surprise, tension, and worry, to name a few.

Raised Brows

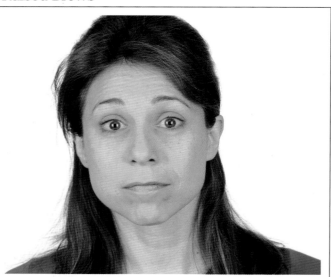

- Raised brows open up the eyes, making them more visible, and can signify openness and interest.

- Alternately, they indicate surprise, especially when the eye brows are raised suddenly and accompanied by a dropped jaw.

- They can also be observed on a questioning face.

- When the raised brow is very strong, the forehead furrows, strengthening a dominant stare or exaggerating a smile.

Lowered Brows

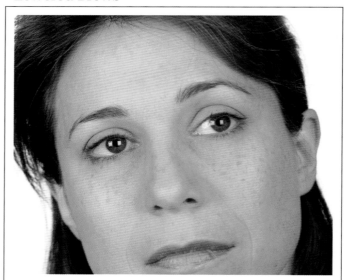

- Lowered eyebrows hide or cover the eyes. They can be indicative of deception.

- They are also induced by annoyance or confusion.

- Lowered brows can even be a sign of dominance because the superior does not want to be annoyed by the inferior.

- If lowered brows are accompanied by a lowered head, the hiding aspect is further used—an alarm bell for deception.

Some women, especially in the days of old, shaved or plucked off the hair of their brows. During some eras women redrew the brows with a pencil to the shape of their preference in order to enhance the beauty of the eyes and face. In Renaissance Florence, Italy, it was the fashion to be without any eyebrow hair at all. The *Mona Lisa*, in fact, doesn't seem to have much contrast on her brows, suggesting no hair. This certainly helps explain why her expression is so perplexing! (She also seems to have no eyelashes.)

Middle, Lowered Brows

- The furrowed brow, or eyebrows that slope downward, most commonly expresses anger.

- The furrowed brow is commonly used in comic books because it caricatures anger.

- The furrowed brow also forms when we want to shield our eyes from bright sun.

- You can carry tension in a furrowed brow without knowing it. Relax the forehead and release the brows to relieve it.

Middle, Raised Brows

- Pushing the eyebrows in and together while lifting the forehead causes the brows to slope up.

- This brow angle signals sadness, but may stay on someone's face even after they are relieved, as emotion is still with them to an extent.

- It can alternately convey anxiety and will be held for as long as the tension lasts.

MICROEXPRESSIONS

You unconsciously flash split-second facial expressions that can give away your feelings

KNACK BODY LANGUAGE

As we will discuss in depth later, differences in cultural background inevitably lead to differences in the way people communicate nonverbally. However, as Dr. Paul Ekman discovered through his objective research, seven emotions show up the same way in every human face and are impossible to hide. All people regardless of culture display the same involuntary facial muscle movements for these emotions.

Ekman began his research by traveling to Papua New Guinea to study the Fore tribesmen. He found that the tribe members not only displayed these hypothesized universal emotions on their own faces but also could recognize and name the emotions on the pictured faces of humans

Anger

- Eyes: Eyes staring could be wide or narrowed; eyebrows pulled down and together.

- Nose/mouth: Nostrils flared; mouth flattened or bottom lip pushing up on top lip or tensely open with teeth clenched and bared.

- Other tells: Chin jutting, or pulled down forehead wrinkled, and face red.

- Note: Anger is shown all over the face, but the most common tell is in the tense and narrowed lips.

Disgust

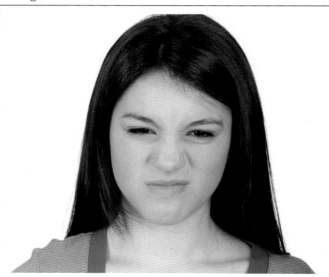

- Eyes: Eyes narrowed; eyebrows pulled down and together.

- Nose/mouth: Nose twisted or scrunched in sneer; mouth closed, possibly with tongue protruding or raised upper lip and protruding lower lip.

- Other tell: Jutting chin.

- Note: Disgust is often confused with anger; tell them apart by the more relaxed (but still expressive) mouth and the nose wrinkle characteristic of disgust but not of anger.

from faraway cultures with which the tribe members had no familiarity. Ekman continued his research with cultures all over the world and found evidence for seven universal emotions, which he termed "microexpressions"—anger, disgust, happiness, sadness, surprise, fear, and contempt. Even when a person tries to hide them, microexpressions flash involuntarily for one-fifteenth to one-twentieth of a second, after which the person is then able to wipe the expression away. The microexpressions are not so fleeting as to avoid detection but do require training to recognize and identify with accuracy.

Happiness

- Eyes: Cheeks up, crow's-feet wrinkles at sides of sparkling eyes; slightly raised eyebrows.

- Nose/mouth: Corners of the mouth lifted (open or closed), possible laughter.

- Other tell: Head level, sometimes up or down if laughing.

- Note: The most important tell is the crow's-feet at the outer corner of the eyes. Only one in ten people can mimic the muscle movements necessary to engage crow's-feet and actually fake a real smile.

Sadness

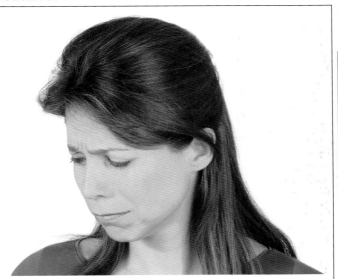

- Eyes: Eyes cast down or losing focus, possibly damp or tearful; upper eyelids drooping; inner eyebrows raised and pulled together.

- Nose/mouth: Lips pinched with corners pulled down; lower lip may push out in a pout.

- Other tell: Head may be down or to the side.

- Note: This is one of the hardest emotions to hide.

MICROEXPRESSIONS (CONT.)

Microexpressions are formed by action units, which are muscle movements of the face

Prior to reading this book, you probably tried to read people, not sure exactly what you were looking for—just kind of intuitively watching. You may have even gotten pretty proficient at it, finding that you "get people". It is likely that one important set of clues you were unconsciously picking up on was microexpressions in the faces of others.

By charting the muscles of the human face and documenting each combination of muscle movements possible in the face, Ekman discovered and named thirty-two distinct action units (AUs). An AU is the contraction or relaxation of one or more muscles. He found that although humans are capable of displaying at least ten thousand emotions, only seven are

Surprise

- Eyes: Eyes wide open; eyebrows raised high and drawn together.

- Nose/mouth: Mouth dropped wide open, subsequently closing within three seconds.

- Other tell: Lifted forehead.

- Note: In an expression of true surprise the eyebrows will raise for only about one second, after which the individual's surprise will turn to a different facial expression, maybe of excitement or fear.

Fear

- Eyes: Eyes wide open; upper lid raised; lower lid tensed; eyebrows raised. Usually we can see the "3 whites" of the eyes, the top and two sides of the white part of our eye.

- Nose/mouth: Mouth open or corners turned down; lips stretched toward ears.

- Other tells: Chin pulled in; head may be slightly back; face pale.

- Note: Fear is often confused with surprise; tell them apart by the eyebrows. In surprise, they are curved, while in fear, they are straight across.

universal, expressed through the same AUs no matter who you are or how good you think you are at hiding your feelings.

Again, the universal emotions, termed "microexpressions," are anger, disgust, happiness, sadness, surprise, fear, and contempt. The first six were established early on, with the seventh universal emotion, contempt, added by Ekman after his later research. It is the only unilateral expression—its tell occurs on only one side of the face. Microexpressions are the only subfield of nonverbal communication that does not require you to gather a baseline before interpreting what they mean.

ZOOM

The "amygdala" plays an important role in recognition of emotional cues. To study generalized social phobia (GSP), researchers compared brain activity of normal individuals with that of people with GSP. When presented with facial expressions of anger or contempt, those with GSP display an abnormally active amygdala, suggesting sensitivity to these two expressions that express disapproval.

Contempt

- Eyes: No specific tell.

- Nose/mouth: One side of the mouth raised and pulled inward into a sneer or smirk.

- Other tell: The head may tilt back so that the person can look down the nose at the object of his or her contempt.

- Note: Contempt is referred to as the "kiss of death" in relationships because those who show it are saying that the other person is inferior, base, or worthless.

NOGGIN NEWS

Microexpressions in Everyday Life

- In order to interpret the meaning of microexpressions, it is not necessary to first baseline an individual.

- When communicating with others, watch for microexpressions in order to gauge your audience's response.

- To adjust for a bad microexpression, use your knowledge of body language to build rapport or ask a direct and open-ended question.

- An example of good question is "It looks to me like something I just said caught you off guard; is that true?"

BEYOND THE MICROS

You also flash more noticeable macroexpressions, which are not universal but learned

You are now well versed on the science behind microexpressions and ready to start looking for them in the faces of those around you. You learned that microexpressions, virtually impossible to fake and largely unconscious, are involuntarily flashed for a microsecond but can then last up to several seconds if the emotion is consciously displayed by the individual. Of course, the human face is capable of expressing many more than just seven emotions, although the other more complex emotions are not shown the same way in all individuals and therefore have larger possibilities for both display and interpretation. The more noticeable and always consciously displayed emotions, called "macroexpressions,"

Startle

- Eyes: Widened eyes; raised eyebrows.

- Nose/mouth: Mouth opens slightly; quick breath may be taken in through nose or mouth.

- Other tells: Lifted forehead; possible audible gasp.

- Note: Although startle and surprise look similar, startle is considered to be more of a reflex to intense sudden stimulation than a reaction to an environmental cue, as in surprise. Startle, like surprise, will quickly turn to the expression of another emotion such as fear, excitement, or relief.

Concentration

- Eyes: Squinted eyes, usually downcast or focused on problem at hand; furrowed eyebrows.

- Nose/mouth: Protrusion of tip of tongue between lips.

- Other tells: Facial strain; head held mostly still until a train of thought is broken.

- Note: The more tells, the higher level of concentration. If the individual has a repetitive habit such as bouncing a leg, this will occur unconsciously, along with diminished perception to outside sights and sounds.

last from one to three seconds and, unlike microexpressions, are heavily influenced by cultural background. What becomes more important when it comes to macroexpressions is the context in which the expressions are present.

Like microexpressions, macroexpressions are identified by somewhat characteristic facial muscle movements, but no one action unit is absolutely essential. Macroexpressions are culturally based and are not scientifically defined, so they do require you to baseline an individual before you attempt to interpret their meaning.

Glaring

- Eyes: Eyes purposely and intensely focused; one eyebrow may be raised.

- Nose/mouth: Nose will wrinkle if disgusted; jaw will clench if angry.

- Other tell: Head raised or pulled back to create distance or pushed close to focused-on individual to create stress and fear.

- Note: A glare can convey strong emotions or stress the importance of a statement or request. Look for microexpressions as well as context clues for the meaning behind the glare.

Anxiety

- Eyes: Eyes damp, unfocused, or closed; eyebrows slightly pushed together.

- Nose/mouth: Trembling of lower lip or biting of either upper or lower lip.

- Other tells: Wrinkled chin; possible brow and forehead sweat.

- Note: Anxiety is a longer-lasting emotion and is psychological as well as physiological, usually affecting other parts of the body— sweaty palms, shaky hands, fidgeting legs, and so forth. The tells are largely dependent on the cause and the individual.

HEAD POSITION

Where's your head? The angle, tilt, and direction of your head can reveal where your mind is

Think about a time when you were told to keep your chin up, to hold your head high, or to lower your head. Many scenarios may have necessitated any one of those three head positions. For instance, your parents may have told you to keep your chin up to increase confidence, to hold your head high to show pride, or to lower your head in respect at a funeral.

The position of the head has a lot to do with an individual's attitude, but because the head is where we gather most our sensory information, it can also reveal where the individual's interest lies. Let's say you want to be perceived as focused, attentive, and interested in something in front of you—would you hold your head down, looking at the ground?

Lowered Head

- **Threatened:** By covering the neck with the chin, one adopts a defensive posture.

- **Submission/respect:** Lowered eyes can be seen as submission, as in "I dare not even look at you," or simply show respect.

- **Flirting:** Maintaining eye contact is a strong flirting signal (typically used by women).

- **Note:** Avoid lowering your head when trying to earn the respect of coworkers and establish yourself as an equal because you will appear submissive and inferior.

Raised Head

- **Superiority/contempt:** It may appear as if the person is looking down his or her nose at those around.

- **Imagination:** Visual thinkers tend to look upward when imagining mental images.

- **Interest:** When the head is only slightly raised, it may be a sign of interest, typically accompanied by raised eyebrows.

- **Note:** A raised head exposes the neck, a very vulnerable body part, but mostly indicates confidence ("You can't hurt me").

Angled toward the window? As ridiculous as it sounds, many people do just this on job interviews and dates, unaware of how their head position is screaming nervousness, indifference, or lack of focus to the interviewer or date.

Just as every body language move has many possible meanings, so does each head position. You must first baseline an individual's head positioning in different situations (listening, speaking, walking) as well as account for cultural variables before interpretation.

NOGGIN NEWS

Tilted Head

- Interest: Tilting the head to the side can be one way to demonstrate interest in what is being said or happening.

- Curiosity: It may indicate curiosity, especially if the head is pushed forward as if to hear or see more.

- Flirting: A woman may tilt her head to purposely expose the neck, which men find attractive.

- Note: When coupled with pulling the head back, a tilted head can indicate suspicion or skepticism.

Nodding

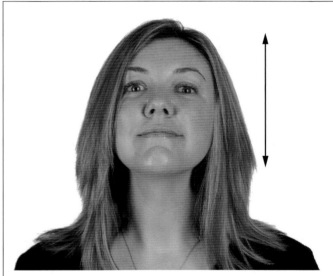

- Agreement: Nodding up and down signals agreement in most cultures; faster head nods indicate stronger agreement.

- Understanding: Nodding slowly while a person is speaking is a good way to show that you are following what he is saying.

- Recognition: A single upward nod shows recognition and typically involves two males; a downward nod may show more respectful recognition.

- Note: Nodding the head up and down signals disagreement in some Middle Eastern cultures.

WHAT THE LIPS SAY

Next to the eyebrows, the lips are the most expressive feature of the face

During verbal communication word formation is governed by how we move our mouth and, more specifically, our lips. In this section you will learn that, in a figurative sense, the lips don't stop talking when words stop coming out. How you hold your lips while listening or doing other activities that don't involve speaking can say a lot.

The lips have special power in the field of dating. Desirable to both men and women, they often capture the attention of your date or person of interest whether you realize it or not. Picture a bar in which you are standing at one end of the room, the individual with whom you are making eye contact at the other. You can send very different messages by

KNACK BODY LANGUAGE

Parted Lips

- Prespeak: During a conversation dominated by one person, you may see the quieter person's mouth open and close several times when trying to interject.

- Flirting: Is a strong flirting signal, particularly if licking the lips while holding the gaze of another person.

- Absentmindedness/concentration: May indicate that a person is "zoned out."

- Note: In a professional setting, parted lips can be perceived as absentminded or sexual and inappropriate.

Pursed Lips

- Tension: Muscles, including muscles in the lips, contract and tighten when an individual is tense.

- Frustration/disapproval: When the lips are pulled in from all directions, they may signal frustration or disapproval.

- Anger: According to micro-expression research, pursed lips are one of the tells of anger.

- Note: Pursed lips often are a sign that the person is holding back her thoughts, as if regrettable words would come out if the mouth opened.

how you hold your lips—slightly open, indicating desire; in the form of a slight smile, conveying approachability and a more playful and innocent desire; in a slight sneer, showing disgust or superiority rather than interest in the individual. No matter the situation, there are strategic ways to hold and move your lips as well as ways to avoid. Because the lips have such a strong sexual connotation, it is especially important to be aware of the signals you are sending.

Puckered Lips

- Flirting: Because men find lips desirable, a woman might pucker around a man she is trying to attract.

- Contemplation: Puckering can indicate uncertainty during thought, particularly if the lips are touched with the fingers.

- Brainstorming: Many people tend to pucker their lips, sometimes to twist them to the side while brainstorming ideas or what to say next.

- Note: When out on the dating scene, women may apply lipstick to enhance and draw more attention to the lips.

Sneered Lips

- Contempt: When one side of the upper lip is pulled upward, this is a microexpression of contempt.

- Disgust: If coupled with a nose wrinkle, sneered lips further the microexpression of disgust.

- Aggression: Sneered lips with bared teeth are a sign of aggression.

- Note: Many animals also show aggression by sneered lips and bared teeth—picture a territorial dog that is ready to attack.

CROSSING

Folding our arms creates a shield from behind which we think, hide, and protect ourselves

Picture this: Today in the office you witness two managers discussing the debacle that unfolded between coworkers at the last company outing. Manager A informs manager B of what she believes should come out of the situation and how the two fighting coworkers should be reprimanded. She is doing most of the talking. Her face is expressive, and her arms are gesturing widely as she leans in toward manager B. Manager B smiles and nods, his arms folded at his chest as he leans away from manager A.

If you were to conclude from this encounter that the two managers were in agreement on the subject matter, you would most likely be wrong. Although manager B is

Interlocking Fingers

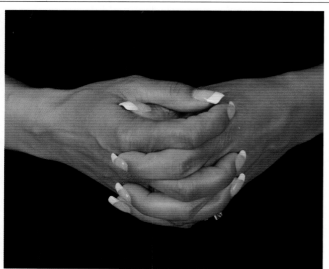

- When a person sits with hands either in one's lap or on a desk, the gesture takes the meaning of obedience and attentiveness.

- This is especially true when accompanied with eye contact and erect posture.

- Interlock your fingers:

- Which thumb lands on top? Now attempt to interlock your fingers with the opposing thumb on top.

- Exercises in properly mimicking interlocking finger patterns have been used to determine parietal lobe dysfunction.

Arms Crossed and Relaxed

- As this may be the most widely discussed body language gesture, by the general public, it can be the kiss of death for a salesperson. This position is one of thought and perseverance.

- We can make ourselves better problem solvers: Cross your arms when faced with a difficult task, and you will convince your brain to work harder to solve it!

- Although this gesture often signifies intense thought or opinion, it can often be read as boredom.

attentively smiling and nodding at manager A, his body language suggests otherwise. With his arms folded at his chest, he is creating a barrier between manager A and himself. He is subliminally signaling that he is not in agreement and not willing to shift his opinion on the matter.

When a person's hands and arms cross, they create a shield from the person with whom the first person is interacting. This shield can function in a variety of ways, from creating a safe place to think to a defensive blockade from attack to a place in which to hide. A person with folded arms has been found to be more persistent in problem solving and more resistant to giving up her position in an argument. The significance of the folding gesture can vary and depends on the accompanying gesture cluster and situation at hand . . . no pun intended.

Crossing arms almost always means something, whether you'd like to admit it or not. In some situations you might think you are crossing your arms to be comfortable or "just because," but examine yourself, and you will find a reason because there rarely is not one.

Crossed Arms Clenching and Squeezing

- Monkeys have been found to use this defensive position when they feel threatened.

- As humans we feel the need to hide behind things. When there is nothing to protect us, such as a chair, wall, or parent, we hide behind our folded arms.

- This is a reassuring posture often used to combat fear, insecurity, anxiety, and vulnerability.

- Salespeople sometimes counter this reserved position by asking the client to hold something or to perform a task involving the hands.

Crossed Arms with Fists

- This is a defensive sign indicating hostility and aggression. The body is often straight, and the chest is puffed up to appear larger.

- With clenched fists, the person is poised to attack.

- The tight fists also hold tension that is being held back.

- Bouncers and unarmed guards often hold this position—when armed, people often feel no need to fold their arms: Their weapon will suffice.

HOLDING

We hold and cradle to comfort ourselves and to ease our frustrations

One of our most comforting memories is a hug from a family member or close friend. As people, we want to hold and to be held, a trait that we were born with. Our social communication is designed around how we gesture to and touch one another.

When you were little, your parent or caregiver would hold you when you were in distress. We continue to display this behavior throughout our lives. Hugging releases oxytocin,

the "love hormone," an instant and natural pick-me-up. It is the same hormone released after sex and during childbirth. When you feel stressed, you crave the comfort of the protecting and reassuring hug of a close one, and so you might take it upon yourself to relieve the stress, frustration, or sadness. You might give yourself a hug.

Well, wrapping your arms around yourself and rocking back and forth might prove socially disastrous. We have therefore

Holding a Wrist

- This position indicates frustration and a level of self-control. The person is potentially restraining this arm to keep from attacking.

- The higher the person holds his arm, the more frustrated he may be.

- This position is used by lawyers in courtrooms as they interview witnesses.

Hands in Front of Groin

- Classic protection gesture: The person is protecting the species' most important and sensitive area of the body from an attack.

- The gesture indicates insecurity and nervousness.

- People often stand in this position when surrounded by strangers.

- Elevators, waiting rooms, and bus stops are perfect places to spot this behavior.

developed more subtle means of achieving the same desired effect. We might grab a wrist or hold one arm at the elbow with the other.

Holding may also imply a holding back or shielding of information. In this way we might hold our arms behind ourselves or place our hands in front of our groin in a protective stance.

Midarm Hold

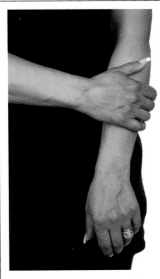

- The arm across the body functions as a shield in the same way a parent holds a child with a single arm around him during a moment of distress.

- This gesture indicates a lack of self-confidence and insecurity.

- This is a ubiquitous gesture seen in cliques of high school girls.

Wrist Hold

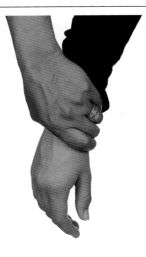

- This gesture is often expressed behind the back.

- Wrist holding displays frustration and self-control.

- The higher the grip, the more frustrated the person is.

- This gesture is often exhibited by people in positions of authority in conversation with one another.

ARMS & HANDS

RUBBING

We calm and reassure ourselves subconsciously by rubbing our head and neck

After a long, hard day at work, nothing seems better than a good back rub. Did you fight with the boss and even get stuck in traffic on the way home? You're probably aching for a massage. We, as humans, want to be touched. From the time we enter the world, we are cuddled, cradled, rocked, stroked, held, and hugged. In fact, physiological, biological,

and social development is dependent upon touch in infancy. When mammals are not touched as infants, they often do not adapt to their environments and are wrought with developmental and communication problems. Humans who were not touched in infancy may even lose the ability to master spoken language. Touch is essential to the development of

Hands Clenching Together

- Although sometimes mistakenly thought to reflect confidence and respect, this gesture often reflects frustration, restraint, and anxiety.

- It can be seen with hands resting in the lap with elbows on chair arms.

- The height of the hands is correlated with the level of frustration the person feels.

- The gesture is often exhibited by debating politicians.

Hands to Neck

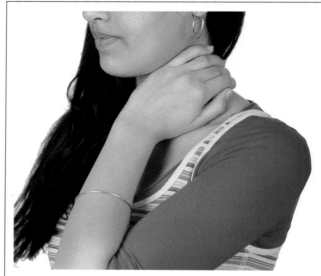

- This gesture is used when a person feels intimidated, threatened, angry, and frustrated.

- The gesture originated as a means to make our fur pelts stand up so we would look larger (similar to goose bumps!).

- This gesture is seen in hospital waiting rooms or business negotiations.

- We rub to comfort ourselves.

92

human communication and interaction.

Our dependency on the touch of our caregivers leaves us primed to find comfort through touch. Rubbing is a product of this. We rub ourselves as a means to comfort ourselves. When we feel stress, anxiety, discomfort, and insecurity, we rub our hands and our necks. We do the same when we feel nervous and unsure of ourselves. This self-pacification through touch reminds us of the care we received in infancy, and so we can use this gesture on ourselves in a variety of ways whenever we need reassurance.

Head and neck gestures, such as rubbing or touching, are very accurate in their indication of the emotion a person is subconsciously communicating. These behaviors are pancultural and occur in real time. These gestures are derived from the limbic system, one of the oldest parts of the brain, which handles, among other things, emotion, behavior, and sense of smell. The person will often have no conscious control of the behaviors. Learning to identify these behaviors will allow you to judge exactly how you or your conversation partner is feeling and if the partner needs extra reassurance or comfort.

Throat

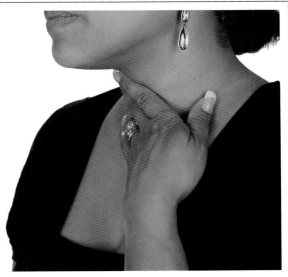

- We touch our collars, necks, and necklaces when we need reassurance.

- Collared shirt wearers might tug at the ends of the collar for the same effect.

- People with long hair may stroke the back of the neck upward, pulling up their hair.

- Pregnant women will rub their belly, protecting and assuaging the fetus, instead of shielding and caressing their own neck.

Palms Together

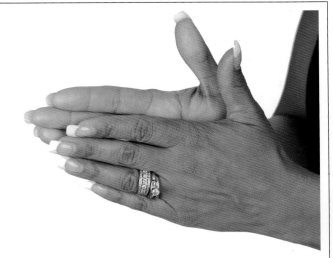

- Rubbing our palms together is a self-massaging and pacifying gesture.

- We often perform this gesture when we are looking forward to something or are impatient about something.

- The rate at which we rub our palms together is correlated with the stress we feel.

- A similar stress behavior is tugging at the skin between our thumb and pointer finger.

HIDING
Hidden hands and concealed mouth give away your secret—well, if you have one

Imagine that you come home and find your four-year-old neighbor standing in your front yard smiling up at you with her hands behind her back. Uh-oh. What has she done this time? Then you notice the pile of freshly cut tulips scattered about her feet, the ones you had planted weeks ago and had impatiently been waiting for to bloom. You ask her what she

is doing, and she responds, "Nothing." She knows she was caught "red handed." What she didn't yet realize was that in hiding her hands behind her back, she had already primed you to suspect her guilt.

If open palms signify openness and submission, a hidden or closed palm shows a level of deceit, discomfort, or dominance.

Thumb in Fist

- Babies tend to keep their hands in fists with the thumbs tucked in. It is not a surprise that this gesture indicates insecurity.

- Thumbs indicate confidence and assertiveness; the more visible and involved they are in conversation, the more confidence

you exude. Rule of thumb: When your thumbs are missing, your confidence is missing as well.

- Although fists are typically aggressive gestures, if you were to punch someone with your thumb inside your fist, you would break your thumb on impact.

Hands behind Back

- Humans like to see hands. When they are hidden, we think something is wrong.

- Hidden hands indicate hidden or withheld information.

- The hands-behind-the-back gesture is used in lying and deceit.

- It is not to be confused with putting the hands behind the back as a means of power.

Like your neighbor, many little kids hide their hands behind their backs when they suspect they have gotten caught doing something bad or are just blatantly lying about something. Adolescents and adults put their hands into their pockets when they feel uncomfortable or out of place. Hiding the palms is another signal. A downward-facing palm shows dominance. This is a control-taking position, used by authority figures, or is simply a sign of superiority. In contrast, open palms are submissive and communicate that you hand over your will, or power, or that you have nothing to hide.

Hands Covering Mouth

- This gesture is used to mask or hide conversation. It is a stereotypical secret-sharing gesture.

- It is used when expressing astonishment or apology.

- People touch their faces around their mouth when they get in trouble and have to explain themselves.

- This gesture indicates that the person has self-doubt, is lying, or is attempting to keep words from escaping his mouth.

Thumbs Hooking Pockets

- Though thumbs are being partially hidden in the pockets, this gesture is more of a display.

- Thumbs indicate dominance, assertiveness, and confidence.

- This is a dominant gesture used to highlight a person's groin and attract attention to it.

- The gesture is often seen when people flirt with one another.

ARMS & HANDS

MESSAGING

We incorporate emblems into our conversations when words alone will not suffice

Here's the scenario: You and some friends snagged some third-row tickets to a rock concert. Toward the end of the concert, your friend waves you down and shouts something to you. You can't hear him, and so you cup your hand behind your ear, leaning toward him. He forms his hand around an invisible cup and makes a drinking motion. You give him a

thumbs up. He brings you back a drink. You are getting tired, so you tap your wrist with the fingers of your other hand. He shrugs and then nods, and you point to the exit. You both head back to the car.

Congratulations. You have had an entire conversation by gesturing. Whereas sign languages communicate entirely

A-okay

- This gesture is done by touching your thumb to your forefinger and fanning out the other three fingers.

- United States: The "a-okay" symbol is a positive gesture in the United States.

- Middle/southern Europe: The gesture means that

the recipient is a zero or a nobody.

- Some Mediterranean countries, Brazil: The gesture takes on a vulgar tone, meaning "a-hole."

Time

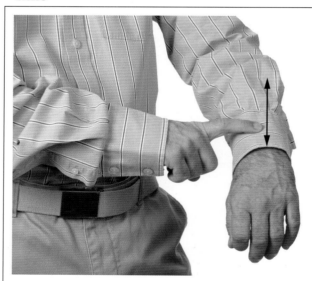

- Most people understand that you are referring to the time when you tap one wrist with the fingers of the other hand.

- You can use other gestures as well as facial expressions to convey what you mean by the gesture.

- You might nod your head toward the exit as you tap your wrist if it is time to leave.

- You may raise your eyebrows or tilt your head if you are silently asking someone for the time.

through a diverse and intricate set of gestures, spoken language relies on a number of nonverbal gestures as well. In spoken language hand gestures can be used to communicate words and phrases in conversation. These gestural substitutes for words and phrases are known as "emblems." They complement conversations and allow people to communicate where speaking might not be appropriate or possible because of distance or environment. Be aware; although most emblems are communicated directly to another person, they may be subtly, unconsciously performed.

ZOOM

Emblems are culturally dictated, and a positive one in your community may not be appropriate to another culture. Notable emblem mishaps: The "thumbs up" emblem, which indicates approval in the United States, is an incredibly vulgar insult in Iran. Similarly, the backward "peace sign" may seem perfectly harmless to Americans, but, in fact, is a vulgar insult in the United Kingdom.

Stop

- Holding your palm vertically facing away from you undeniably means "stop."

- This gesture is what is called an "emblem"—a signal that is understood the same way by nearly every person.

- Because of its universality, the stop signal is used by police officers when directing traffic.

- Although the signal to stop is universal, what it is referring to is contextual—it could be a request to stop talking, don't come any closer, and so forth.

Crazy Person

- When you twirl your pointer finger next to one temple or ear in a circular motion, you are saying the person referred to is crazy.

- The circular twirl next to the head mimics taking a screw from the head; it comes from the expression "that person has a screw loose."

- This signal indicating "crazy" is most often referred to as an "emblem" because most people understand it this way.

- In Argentina, however, this signal means "You have a phone call."

ILLUSTRATING

Illustrated speech is designed to aid the speaker more than it is the listener

We are visual creatures. We rely heavily upon our sense of sight to understand the world around us. When our words alone cannot suffice in conversation, our hands step in and complete our thoughts.

If someone were to ask you directions, you would probably give the directions and also use your hands to indicate which direction to go, which way to turn, and so forth. In fact, you might signal right or left with your hands in giving directions, even if you were talking on the phone.

These gestures not only are used for communication but also are important to our own cognition. In other words, gesturing as a means of describing is just as important to

Right/Left Turn

- Just motioning to the right or the left has no distinct meaning.

- Unlike an emblematic gesture when messaging, no conventional definitions exist for illustrating gestures—without words or context they can mean anything.

- The person in the image may be giving someone directions. In that context the motions make sense.

- Motioning right or left reiterates the directions and provides a visual guide.

Tying the Shoe

- This hand-over-hand motion means nothing without a context.

- But say it is being done while teaching a child to tie a shoe.

- Suddenly the gesture becomes an illustrator, exemplifying how an imaginary shoe would be tied.

- Again, illustrators are great gestures to use as guides or teaching aides.

the speaker as it is to the listener. The listener will gather the same information from the speaker whether or not he can see the speaker's explicit gestures.

The act of gesturing greatly impacts the mind and improves vocabulary. There is a correlation between childhood language development and the broader variety of gesture use. When we communicate, we involve our entire bodies, and so it is no surprise that gesturing is an important part to our language development and our communication efficiency.

Size of the Fish

- Holding the hands apart at any given distance has no intrinsic meaning.

- Let's put the gesture into context. The person in the image is illustrating the size of a fish he caught the other day.

- With words: "It was a big one! Two feet, like this."

- Though it has no distinct meaning, the gesture is generally used to illustrate measurement and to visualize size.

Climbing a Ladder

- Pulling the hands down one after the other does not have one given definition.

- However, it may be recognized as a motion that mimics, or illustrates, climbing a ladder.

- It may be used to illustrate a literal example of climbing a ladder.

- Or it may be used to illustrate the idioms of climbing the social ladder or the career ladder.

ARMS & HANDS

99

HEAD TO TOES

Humans have less conscious control over body parts farthest from their brain

It is an interesting exercise to watch the body language of a small child in the middle of a fib. She will play nervously, almost fanatically, with her arms and legs while trying to maintain a serious face. Adults, too, albeit to a lesser degree, often give themselves away when lying, not by their facial expression but rather by nervous toe taps or unintentional limb movements. The reason? The farther a body part is from the brain, the less control humans have over it; thus, it is relatively easier to control what the face is doing than the legs.

Knowing this can be used to your advantage in a number of ways: You can know to be aware of other people's feet when doubting their sincerity, and you can better try to

KNACK BODY LANGUAGE

Toes Pointing Inward

- The pointing in of the feet is a sign of subservience and vulnerability.

- Females often sit with their toes pointed inward when in a romantic setting to display submissiveness and innocence.

- This is viewed as a weak stance and is avoided in professional settings where confidence and dominance are valued.

- Many people associate this stance with humiliation because it is the stance children take when they realize they are about to have "an accident."

The Pointer

- A person in an uncomfortable situation may have his feet and legs pointed toward an exit.

- This is a strong indicator that he wants to leave, meaning the feet will tell the body where to go.

- The feet may also point toward another individual if that is where the person's interest lies.

- In couples, the less-interested partner often has his legs pointing away from the other partner in social settings, indicating a desire to escape.

control your own feet lest they give you away! This means that although most advanced card players know to throw a tablecloth over glass tables to prevent the reflection from giving away their hand, they may not know that another advantage is to cover their feet from giving away what their face is trying to hide. In other words, it is much easier to have a poker *face* than poker *legs*.

What to Look For

- If someone's face, hands, or upper extremities are not revealing much about her state of mind, look to the legs and feet.

- Look for shoes, sandals, or heels being balanced off the tip of the toes or slipped on and off.

- Look for "toe play" such as curling, wiggling, and clenching.

- Look at the angle of the knees—inward or outward. Look at the direction legs move—when crossed, are they bouncing in circles or staying still?

The Seated Runner

- The feet receive the least amount of attention from the brain, but this changes when the body is in fight-or-flight mode.

- A threatened or uncomfortable person will sit with hands slightly propping his body up and one foot forward so that he can quickly spring up and fight or flee if necessary. Clenched fists accompanying this position indicate a desire to fight.

- Fight-or-flight can be observed as a frozen gesture because some people in high-stress situations tend to simply freeze and maintain the pose.

THE WAY WE WALK

The way we walk can hold implicit messages about the person we try to portray ourselves as

Have you noticed how a man develops a wider-set gait at a relatively fast pace when he is trying to impress a woman? This is in effort to exude strength, health, and vigor. When we see someone taking confident, long, springy strides, we unconsciously attribute certain characteristics to that person: healthy, confident, youthful.

A person can choose many ways to enhance his or her walk, all of which convey different messages about what that individual is trying to portray. Someone who tries to appear sexy may keep touching her neck and arms while walking with exaggerated slow steps, just as someone who tries to appear deep in thought may walk with decisive, quick steps

Folded Arms Walk

- Walking while the arms are folded generally suggests the person is in a protective and defensive mode (both men and women, depending on the situation).

- Arms can be tightly folded, clutching the body, or even loosely wrapped around the body.

- This position indicates feelings of uncertainty, apprehension, anxiousness, and lack of confidence.

- Wrapping the arms around the body can be very comforting because it mimics the feelings of being hugged or held.

Hands-in-the-pocket Walk

- Generally this walk may indicate an introverted individual; it can also suggest concealing feelings from others while still feeling judgmental of others.

- This position may denote feelings of depression, especially if accompanied by a slow-paced walk, caused by frustration or anger.

- The position can be used by people who know they tend to fidget when nervous as a way to keep their hands controlled. One hand in the pocket, conversely, is seen as a sign of being laidback and relaxed.

102

and a furrowed brow. Although it is true that walking in itself is quite basic on the scale of body language behaviors—just one foot in front of the other—the nuances a person throws into her walk can make this seemingly simple act quite complex in terms of implied body communication.

Arm movements, facial expressions, and posture can add a lot to a person's walk, and each element should be looked at individually and holistically in order to capture what the individual's walk says about the character she tries to portray.

Deep Thoughts Walk

- This walk includes bowing the head and often gazing at the ground with unfocused eyes.

- It looks similar to the hands-in-the-pocket walk because the pace is also slow, but in this case the person is trying to concentrate on his thoughts.

- Commonly the person will walk back and forth across a specific space but not to reach any particular destination.

- Facial features include furrowing the brows or biting the lip.

Strutting Walk

- This walk can include a stiff and inflexible posture with the chin raised to project a proud and superior image.

- The individual may artificially push out the chest and swing arms with an exaggerated movement.

- This walk signals a great degree of control and is generally associated with a person having an arrogant and egoistic character.

- The exaggerated male strut is the army march, whereas the exaggerated female strut is the runway catwalk.

STANDING LEGS
A person's stance can tell a great deal about his comfort level

Although it may seem easier to read another person's body language when she is engaged in dramatic hand gestures or elaborate foot maneuvering, the simple act of standing can also tell a lot about how secure or comfortable a person feels as well as how engaged or interested she is in remaining where she is.

All of the previously discussed standards of closed versus open body language signals apply here as well: Crossed arms and legs are closed positions that signify hesitance, anxiety, or discomfort, whereas relaxed arms and legs are open positions that signify ease and comfort. This is a circular process in that a person may stand with crossed legs and arms because she feels uncomfortable and insecure, but her stance will cause others to perceive her as uncomfortable and standoffish. Therefore, they will interact less with her, adding to her feelings of discomfort and causing her to

KNACK BODY LANGUAGE

Crossed Legs

- This stance is typical when someone is introduced to a group for the first time and unsure of what will happen next.

- This position may indicate shyness and apprehension, and the legs are literally hugging each other for support.

- Stance may be accompanied by arms crossed in front of the body, and the head may be in a lowered position for ultimate closed-off display.

- This is an unstable position, so this is seldom a defensive stance, although it can be submissive.

Open Legs

- Holding the legs approximately shoulder width apart while standing is a stable stance in a normally relaxed pose.

- The person indicates that he or she feels grounded and confident.

- Standing with a purpose-ful, wider stance makes the body appear wider (bigger) and signals a feeling of dominance as the person takes up more space.

- An open-leg stance does display and make vulnerable the genitals. This can be a sexual display or a show of power.

maintain her stance. Being aware of this fact is important if you find yourself in the uncomfortable position of being at an event where you don't know anyone. You can try to "fake" comfort by standing with a relaxed stance, thus inviting contact and conversation from others.

Closed Legs

- A person standing with feet together or closer than a relaxed shoulder width may indicate a feeling of anxiety.

- This stance makes the person seem smaller as a target, gives some protection to the genitals, and is a display of cautiousness.

- A fully closed standing position with knees touching indicates an increased desire for protection.

- In variants of this position, the person may be turned slightly to the side, leaning forward a little, or pulling the hips back.

Alternate Standing Positions

- The one-leg-up stance: Leaning against a wall with one leg bent back at the knee and a foot resting behind on the wall is the embodiment of "cool."

- The crossed-ankle stance: Crossing your ankles makes you look like you have urgency to use the restroom. Avoid it.

- The hip lean: Bearing more weight on one leg than the other causes the hip to tilt and is often used when waiting or when feet are tired.

LEGS & FEET

SEATED LEGS
Seated positions can tell us much about displays of masculinity, femininity, and openness

In general people tend to feel more comfortable at social gatherings when they are allowed to be seated. When you are seated, less of your body is "on display," and the nervous tells that are easy to detect when standing, such as fidgeting and arm and leg movements, are less obvious when sitting.

That said, a wealth of body language information still comes through from analyzing the way a person is seated. Many signs of masculinity or femininity come through depending on the style in which a person's legs are positioned. Basic knowledge of human anatomy will allow you to analyze why it is considered the ultimate alpha seating position for a man to have his legs spaced far apart or one leg crossed at

Open Legs

- Sitting with slightly open legs is a naturally relaxed position indicating the person is comfortable and at ease.

- One or both legs may be dropped down sideways if the person is really comfortable.

- Men tend to sit with a relaxed, wider opening of the legs, and this can be even more of a sexual "crotch display." Some people may be subconsciously aware of this and may let their hands drop between their legs to cover the genitals.

Crossed Ankles

- Crossing the ankles displays a relaxed position, especially when the person's legs are stretched out in front and the body is leaning back with or without hands cupping the head. If, however, the person's hands are clenched with crossed ankles, this is a sign of self-restraint.

- An ankle cross with legs tucked under the body may indicate concealed anxiety, especially when the person is leaning forward.

- Males tend to sit in those positions with legs far apart and meeting only at the ankles, whereas women will have legs close together.

a 90-degree angle with the crossed leg lying parallel to the floor—it is a display of phallic dominance. This is also why it is uncommon for a woman, even if she is wearing trousers, to sit in either of these positions unless she is purposefully trying to display masculinity and dominance.

The differences in seating positions are seen in terms of not only gender but also culture. Different cultures have different rules about what is appropriate seating, and what is considered casual seating in one culture may be seen as a direct insult in another.

Crossed Legs: In General

- Crossed legs can indicate a closed mind stemming from fear, anxiety, or defensiveness.

- In social situations a woman's crossed legs don't necessarily mean she's not interested. Women tend to cross legs when wearing skirts.

- In America men tend to cross their legs with a wide stance with the top crossed leg parallel to the ground. This is "crotch display"—a signal of power.

- If both the legs and the arms are crossed, this is the ultimate signal of being closed off to contact from others.

Crossed Legs: Sex

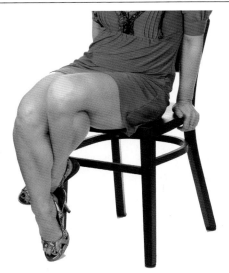

- A relaxed crossing of the legs may be used as a sexual signal by a woman, particularly if her legs are exposed.

- Some women entwine their legs in an attempt to draw attention to the well-developed muscle tone of their legs.

- Men who want to flirt may sit with legs crossed at a wide angle to provide a display of masculinity.

- A very feminine flirting display is tightly crossing legs and sitting at an angle. Men biologically cannot sit in this position and tend to find it highly attractive.

FEET: WHERE TO GO

The direction the feet point also indicates where interest points

Because the farther from the brain body parts are, the less conscious control of them we have, the feet often give away where our true attention is directed. Although you may be faking total engrossment in a dull conversation with eye and head contact, chances are your feet are tapping impatiently or pointing toward an exit.

If you are stuck in a situation in which you feel bored or anxious to get to other things, you may find your feet tapping away or engaging in quick jerks—this is your body's way of preparing you for your getaway so that you can spring up and walk away when you detect the first opportunity when it is socially acceptable to do so.

If you want to find out if a conversation partner is really interested in what you are saying, looking at her legs and feet can give a better indication than trying to read her facial expressions. It is much easier to feign interest with head nods

Pointing

- We tend to point at things that are of interest to us with our hands and even our feet.

- Foot pointing is more subtle and often not noticed compared with facial or hand movements.

- The feet point the way to go and send signals about people we like or places we want to go. Swinging the foot can be a form of pointing.

- Bored feet point away from the boring converser and toward another person or place the person would rather be close to.

Stamping

- Stamping makes a noise and can be an attention-getting signal, as in saying, "Hey! Listen to me!"

- Stamping one foot is often used to indicate anger or aggression and is commonly seen in little children who are throwing a tantrum.

- People stamp their feet in conjunction with shouting in an attempt to frighten another person or gain a person's attention quickly.

- In many cultures, such as Israeli and Palestinian, stamping the feet is part of the traditional dance.

and an affected smile than it is to realize that anxious feet are tapping away or pointing toward a more interesting conversation partner. These signs can be an indication for you to adjust the conversation before your partner gets even more bored or restless.

Shaking/Tapping

- Tense, repetitive movements such as tapping the foot can be a sign of impatience or boredom.

- People are often unaware that they are shaking or tapping their feet.

- The foot literally becomes like a clock's pendulum, marking and moving in time, and can signify a desire to speed up time and end the present interaction.

- Moving the feet is also a common indicator of lying, particularly if the person is sitting down with feet hidden under a table.

Fun Foot Facts

- Some people roll their feet in circles on the balls of their ankles.

- This behavior can express either relaxation or contemplation. It may also be habit. Many people do it while lounging and reading.

- Feet and shoe choice tell a lot about a person.

- Are the shoes or feet clean or dirty? Are the nails manicured or not? Does the person have a preference for athletic shoes, comfortable shoes, or stylish shoes?

FOOT PLAY

It's not all serious when dealing with the legs; many playful and flirtatious exchanges involve the feet!

Although the feet don't typically come to mind when thinking of erogenous zones, the feet can be surprisingly erotic. We tend to associate the feet with practical purposes: walking, running, moving to get us from point A to point B. But mixing in flirtatious moves and a practical body part in a flirty game such as "footsie" can be quite romantic, too.

In fact, because of their high practical demand, the feet are home to many nerve endings. These prove the practical purpose of warning against injury, but the high concentration of nerve endings on the soles of the feet also means that getting your feet touched can be pleasurable. In fact, the feet are one of the top erogenous zones on the human body.

Erotic Object

- The foot can be an erotic object, and stroking it can be mildly suggestive.

- Accessories to the feet, such as painted toenails, toe rings, anklets, and high-heeled shoes, can enhance the sexual appeal of feet.

- The feet are highly sensitive because of the high concentration of nerve endings.

- Overstimulating the soles of the feet can be uncomfortable.

Massage

- When legs are crossed, the foot may be massaged or squeezed, perhaps to relieve tension or to provide a substitute for massaging tension elsewhere in the body.

- Pregnant women are often in pain because of the added pressure on their feet and can find foot massages especially welcome.

- Foot massages are usually done using circular motions with the inside of the fingers because light taps with the tips of the fingers may tickle.

- Individually massaging the toes is recommended to de-stress the feet.

There is also something vulnerable about allowing someone else to touch your feet. Whereas a person may not think twice about shaking hands with a stranger, it is quite an intimate act to allow yourself to touch someone else's feet or to have your own feet touched. In fact, washing someone else's feet is a common religious or spiritual ritual in many cultures because it shows your absolute humility and closeness.

Footsie

- Footsie is a flirting game between two dating people in which one touches the feet or legs of the other, usually under a table or in hidden manner.

- Sometimes the game involves kicking each other playfully.

- Often the game is given away by facial expressions such as laughter.

- The secrecy of footsie can make it a very intimate way for two people to express contact and interest without others around them knowing.

Foot Anatomy

- Why are feet so ticklish? The feet have so many nerve endings that the feet become highly sensitive to touch.

- All these nerve endings provide feedback to the brain in order to help us judge how to step.

- Some people walk with their feet pointing in (in-toeing). People also walk with their feet pointed out (out-toeing), which causes them to waddle a bit like a duck.

- These are abnormalities and can be corrected with orthotics.

THREE AREAS
Explore how space influences communication, situations, and relationships

The anthropologist Edward T. Hall developed the idea of proxemics, or the study of space, in the mid-1960s. More specifically, proxemics can be defined as the study of the relationship between spatial distance and interaction of individuals. The distances that individuals place between themselves and others are dependent on a variety of variables.

Proxemics describes three types of space: fixed-feature space, semifixed-feature space, and informal space. Fixed-feature space describes immovable areas such as the ground, walls, and the ceiling of an office. When talking about fixed-feature space, you are implying that something is permanent. Many individuals disagree on what is considered fixed and

Fixed-feature Space

- Immovable features, such as the ceilings and walls of a room, provide clear boundaries of where a space starts and ends.

- People often organize activities in relation to fixed-feature space, so the walls of a classroom encompass a boundary for learning.

- A change in fixed-feature norms, such as trying to hold a meeting in an open field, can lead to discomfort and resistance.

- Fixed-feature space is the top-level deciding factor that sets the boundaries for human behaviors.

Semifixed-feature Space

- Movable objects, such as furniture, can have important implications for how people behave. An example of this fact is walking into a classroom with chairs positioned in a circle; this arrangement can lead to a sense of openness and elicit conversation.

- Sociopetal spaces are semi-fixed features that promote collaboration, such as chairs placed near each other.

- Sociofugal spaces are semi-fixed features that promote separation, such as small chairs spaced out back to back.

what is unfixed. As a guest in someone's home, for example, be cautious about pulling up chairs or moving them around because your host may intend for those chairs to have permanent residency in one specific area. Semi-fixed features are movable features, such as furniture, that can go into that fixed space. Observe how people interact with furniture, if they touch it or where they stand in relation to it. Informal space is the actual personal space around an individual. Proxemics allows you to observe how individuals negotiate with these three different spaces in order to achieve a sense of equilibrium, or balance, with their surroundings.

People can handle these different types of space, especially informal space, very differently depending on their culture or background. Although many of the rules about these spatial norms are unspoken, they are incredibly important to individuals' sense of territory and personhood, and people can feel physically invaded when these norms are not followed.

Informal Space

- This is the "personal space" we feel is necessary around us to keep us comfortable.

- This space is often unconscious because people do not think about the personal space they need to feel at ease but simply adjust to maintain it.

- Different cultures have different ideas of what is appropriate personal space.

- If you are encroaching on someone's personal space, he will make changes, such as stepping back or taking a seat down, in order to feel comfortable.

Exceptions to Spatial Rules

- Some researchers have described groups of people, such as nomadic tribes, for whom the usual norms of fixed-feature space do not apply.

- Individuals may manipulate traditionally semifixed features to become fixed features; for example, an individual may stake claim to a chair, making it "his chair," which he then uses to display ownership and a territorial boundary.

- The rules of informal space norms do not apply in all situations; most people would not make their dentist maintain their usual personal space norms.

113

FIVE ZONES

Personal space holds an important psychological significance in territorial rights for human beings

"I really feel as human beings, we need more training in our basic social skills. Conversational distance: Don't you hate these people that, when they talk to you, they talk into your mouth like you're a clown at a drive-through?" Jerry Seinfeld begins episode 82 of the American sitcom *Seinfeld* with these lines, referring to a character he terms a "close-talker" for his inability to respect social space norms. Although the rules surrounding appropriate distances to keep between oneself and others are not usually explicitly expressed, they are an important aspect of social interaction and can cause much discomfort if ignored.

Personal space is a physical surrounding region that

Intimate Space

- Close intimacy: Less than 6 inches. Far intimacy: 6 to 18 inches.

- This is territorially the most important space to human beings and most protectively kept.

- This is a space reserved for intimate moments with partners, children, and close friends.

- It is a social mistake to attempt to come into someone's intimate space before she feels comfortable with you, which is why it's often advised to move slowly when unsure.

Personal Space

- Close personal space: 18 inches to 2 feet. Far personal space: 2 to 4 feet.

- This is the space we require when engaging in friendly conversations with people we know and/or are comfortable with.

- Depending on cultural context, a stranger may start to feel uncomfortable if you stand in this space.

- If you feel comfortable, light touches on the arm to show connection or solidarity are sometimes appropriate at this distance.

individuals feel "belongs" to them; individuals may lash out and react with offense, defensiveness, or even anger if they feel that this personal region is invaded. Of course, different situations call for different space norms, and the distance that an individual feels comfortable with when speaking to a significant other will be different than the distance the same individual deems necessary for speaking with a group of strangers. Personal space is a psychologically significant concept, with individuals attaching much importance to these invisible boundaries that they regard as rightfully their space.

ZOOM

Psychologist Robert Sommes has explored the mechanisms by which individuals justify violations into their personal space zones, such as imagining that the many bodies squished close to them on the subway are merely inanimate objects. Doing this can reduce the anxiety associated with having so many people at such a close proximity.

Social Space

- Close space: 4 to 7 feet. Far space: 7 to 12 feet.

- This is an appropriate space to give strangers or people you have only recently met.

- In certain contexts you may remain in the social space even if you see the person

every day, for example, the postman.

- In some cultures that value closeness, standing at this distance may be off-putting or offensive and read as a sign you do not want to be standing near that person.

Public Space

- Close phase: 12 to 25 feet. Far phase: 25 feet or more.

- This is an appropriate distance for talking to a group or giving a lecture.

- Hand motions, eye contact, and smiling can help your audience build rapport with

you even if you are standing at the public space.

- This may be too far in smaller rooms or big rooms with small audiences, which may feel too removed from you to pay attention.

IN THE ZONE

When your space overlaps another's, how do you act?

People brought up in the country are used to wide, open spaces. They may easily become claustrophobic in cities or crowds and tend to keep greater distances during social interaction. Their personal space may be a much larger zone than that of a person coming from a crowded metropolitan city. When shaking hands, a city person will walk into the social zone, perhaps even stepping into the personal space, to shake hands. A country person, on the other hand, may keep his feet planted in the public or social space, bend his body in, outstretch an arm to its full capacity, and maybe even lift one foot just to get a little extra reach across that vast space to shake hands.

Within these zones, other aspects of body language besides physical contact, such as handshaking, must be regulated. Speech volume, for example, can breach a spatial boundary. Loud volume in an intimate space translates as someone

Speech Volume

- Adjust the volume of your voice in accordance with the space between you and others.

- The closer you are to people's ears, the lower the volume of your voice. The farther, the louder.

- If you speak too softly across a space and others cannot hear you, you may be perceived as submissive and timid.

- Consider people with hearing aids. Also consider spatial environment. You will have to speak more loudly or softly, depending on your surroundings.

Physical Contact

- When you touch someone, you are immediately entering that person's intimate space.

- Hugging and embracing are acceptable among friends, family, and couples.

- If you are a "hugger" by nature, don't overdo it. Not everyone is comfortable with you inviting yourself into his or her intimate space.

- As acquaintances become friends, they may allow each other into their intimate spaces.

116

screaming in your face—certainly not pleasant. Eye contact, in a way, can also permeate spatial boundaries. We generally don't stare someone in the eye when we are crammed against them on a jam-packed subway. Talk about awkward invasion of personal boundaries. Finally, there is the angle at which our shoulders meet. Is it at an angle open enough to allow others into the space? This is the sociopetal-sociofugal axis.

Eye Contact

- Eye contact in close proximity between strangers can feel awkward for some.

- If you are standing extremely close to a stranger who is making eye contact, it is possible that you won't want to return the eye contact unless you plan on engaging in conversation.

- Eye contact can be used across a space to grab someone's attention.

- How many times have you looked across a space purposefully trying to make eye contact with a waiter?

Sociopetal-Sociofugal Axis

- This axis defines the relationship of the angle of one person's shoulders to another's.

- There are face-to-face, 45-degree, 90-degree, 135-degree, 180-degree, and back-to-back.

- In the above image, the spatial orientation of the two individuals on the left conveys isolation, awkwardness, and disinterest between the two. Their arms are crossed, closing them off from interaction, and they are standing side by side. If they were engaged in conversation, they would probably be angled toward each other.

117

SURROUNDINGS

What's in your space? Notice how objects and surroundings influence body language

So far in this chapter we've talked about distances of empty space. Now let's describe the contents of the space. What are the surroundings and the objects filling and defining the space? Walls close a space in; furniture divides the space; doors regulate the flow of people into the space; windows show other space; and lights illuminate the space. When it comes to proxemics in body language, these items can be used to manipulate space and zones. For example, how do you put a stranger into someone's personal space without breaching his boundaries? Put a wall between them! Hence, we have cubicles, queue dividers at airports, or signs that tell you to wait behind them until you are called, such as at front desks.

Owning a Person/Object

- By placing a hand on this woman's chair, the man shows a certain amount of ownership over the woman.

- It could be that he is a possessive spouse, or he wants to make it clear to all that this woman is his intended territory.

- Or it could mean he is about to engage in conversation with the woman. By touching or holding the chair, he is trying to "own" or possess her attention.

- The move can have multiple interpretations. Look for body language clusters to understand his intentions.

Owning the Room

- By leaning on the door frame, you become boss of the entrance and exit.

- All must pass by your overseeing eye, and you display control over the flow into and out of the room.

- Of course, you are not really controlling anyone, but you do appear as a tollbooth, and you may be perceived as extremely self-assured or, at worst, cocky.

- Drop the gatekeeping if you don't want to appear rude, overbearing, or controlling, even if unintended.

Touching objects, such as leaning on a desk or leaning in a doorway, shows ownership of the space or power over the space. By blocking an exit, for example, you show ownership over the area. You are the "bouncer" deciding or overseeing who comes in and who goes out.

You can tell when someone feels uncomfortable in a space. He will automatically find an object or piece of furniture to touch, lean against, sit on, or simply stand near. Hanging out in empty space, some individuals may feel vulnerable or exposed.

MAKE IT EASY

When hosting a party, arrange the furniture in a fashion that is conducive to social interaction. Too many objects and furniture can create a hectic maze that blocks easy communication between people. Too few objects or not enough chairs to relax in, and your guests may become aimless drifters. Sectioning out areas allows for successful socialization.

Don't Get Too Comfortable

- Leaning on or touching someone's desk is another way of showing ownership.

- Not only are you entering the person's personal space, but also you are claiming territory to it!

- It may be okay with a colleague, but don't try it with the boss's desk.

- In other words, don't get too comfortable unless the situation is comfortable. You can lean on things without appearing possessive in certain scenarios; it all depends on context.

Placing Yourself

- How do you use space to place yourself in the ideal location?

- At a bar you may want to invite socialization or attract romantic interests.

- If this is the case, do not hide and huddle in your space or hunch over the bar closing yourself off.

- Lean sideways on the bar or keep your back to the bar so that you attract some attention to yourself and show that you are open and willing to engage.

AUTHORITY & SPACE

Whoever owns the space owns the interaction; where do you stand?

Authority can be commanded by using space. Think of how many leaders present themselves in their surrounding space. Usually there is a larger distance between them and their inferiors. They will stand on a stage or a heightened area that raises them above others. Doing this gives them an "untouchable quality" and separates them from the rest. Some leaders who are more liberal and want to appeal to the masses will mingle among people and share personal and social space

with them in order to convey that they are on the same page and have similar goals and attitudes. These leaders can be highly popular.

In general, however, leaders, bosses, and people in positions of authority will place extra distance between themselves and their subordinates. If not, subordinates will be aware of their authority and will create the extra space for them.

Spatial Hierarchy

- It is likely that a boss will place more space between himself and subordinates.

- He may do this in order to promote authority and respect.

- Rather than a far personal space of 2 to 4 feet, he may maintain social space of 4

to 7 feet or an even wider social space of 7 to 12 feet. He may use the public space.

- As with a leader addressing the masses, extra space distinguishes the boss and delineates the hierarchy.

Social Space

- Members of the same group will talk noticeably closer to one another.

- Because of their familiarity and bond of sharing mutual power levels, they don't feel the need to use space.

- Groups may include executives, subordinates, coaches, and team players.

- Groups will share personal space and usually won't go beyond the social space.

It is not uncommon to see subordinates literally clearing a path for their boss when he walks down the hall.

Spatial hierarchy really becomes apparent when authority figures and subordinates gather into groups and form shapes. For example, individuals will stand in a horseshoe formation around their boss when he addresses them. Or subordinates will form rows or lines. Think of military gatherings to exemplify this trend.

Sharing Space

- When individuals are speaking, and another party wants to enter the conversation, the other party will step into the space created between the others.

- Stepping into the space is an assertive act and, when accompanied by a hand on the shoulder or arm, shows authority.

- The intruder, whether welcome or not, may want to take charge of the conversation.

- The others will move to make the appropriate space for this assertive individual.

Speaker Space

- You know you've got authority when your audience maintains an organized position in the surrounding space.

- A filed line or seated rows organize the public space.

- The speaker can command the attention of this organized audience by being able to look at the people one by one or to sweep his eyes across the rows.

- If the audience is a scattered, disorganized crowd, it may detract from the command and authority of the speaker.

ATTRACTION SIGNALS

The signals that humans give when feeling attraction are predictable and relatively easy to spot

Humans, like other animals, exhibit tell-tale signs that they feel attraction for another individual. Although you may have been told that there is no science when love is concerned, it turns out there just may be! We undergo a series of sequential and predictable physiological changes when we are attracted to another individual, and learning to spot these can be a valuable tool to have in your dating toolkit.

Main attraction signals include making eye contact, touching, smiling, and preening. After recognizing these more basic signals is mastered, you can try spotting subtler signals, such as self-touching, which is an often-missed signal that someone is interested in you.

KNACK BODY LANGUAGE

Eye Contact

- Making eye contact is an important initial flirting signal.

- Women often must repeat cycles of making eye contact, dropping it, and repeating contact several times for a man to realize she is interested.

- Have you heard of "bedroom eyes"? "Bedroom eyes" refers to dilated pupils, which signify attraction and interest.

- When you look deeply into your lover's eyes, you are unconsciously looking for pupil dilation.

Preening/Self-adjusting

- Preening, or a type of "self-grooming," has been researched by psychiatrist Dr. Albert Scheflen.

- When trying to attract a mate, a man will stand taller, puff out his chest, suck in his gut, and tense his facial muscles to appear more youthful.

- A woman will push out her chest to show off her breasts, suck in her waist, accentuate her hips, and tense her facial muscles to exude vitality.

- This self-adjusting is primarily unconscious.

Although men and women typically give off the same attraction signals, women (and some gay men) exhibit some signals distinct from those of straight men. These signals are meant to signify submissiveness and include displaying widened eyes, sideways glances, and limp wrists and positioning the self to be physically lower than the object of interest so you have to look up to make eye contact. Being aware of these signals is increasingly important in our hectic, fast-paced lifestyles. So as not to miss any potential romantic matches, be aware of the signals you are spotting *and* giving off.

Touch

- Touching someone's hand while talking to him promotes intimacy and closeness.

- Lightly touch the other's hand or arm and watch for a reaction; if the person pulls back or flinches, he or she is not comfortable enough for further touching.

- Self-touch is meant to pique another's interest: Women often play with their hair, legs, or arms in order to activate attraction and draw attention to their bodies.

- Self-touching can be a safe way to hint to another that you are open to physical intimacy.

Smile

- Smiles can be one of the first indicators to show interest.

- Women often give off quick, subtle smiles to draw in attention. A man may need a few tries to notice smiles directed at him.

- A subtle smile can be accompanied by a slightly raised shoulder and tilted head to convey coy submissiveness.

- Attractive smiles exaggerate gender differences: Women can pout to show full lips, and men can clench the jaw slightly to show a strong jaw.

123

BAR MOVES

Obvious displays of dating and mating body language can be found in the bar scene

Although the general rule is that only after people are emotionally comfortable with each other will they stand close together, the crowded bar scene can act like a fast-forward button for normal conventions of closeness and proximity. Bars and nightclubs can be especially tricky places to navigate body language correctly because lowered inhibitions and cramped spaces can make for some awkward moments.

That said, for those who do want to meet and mingle, bars and clubs can be a great way to jump right in. Succeeding in this environment is like conducting a delicate balancing act in which you need to know when to proceed and when to back off. Recognizing what signs indicate interest as

KNACK BODY LANGUAGE

Get Close Enough to Get Noticed

- One of the most common mistakes that singles on the bar scene make is simply not getting close enough to catch anyone's eye.

- Do not spend the whole night hidden away in a corner surrounded by friends. Remember: Groups can be intimidating.

- Stand with open body positions (arms uncrossed, back straight) with legs and body slightly leaning toward the target of interest.

- Navigate the area to make sure you are aware of all your surroundings . . . and potential dates!

Look at That Glass!

- Singles can touch the rim or stem of their glass slowly to prime erotic feelings and the sense of being touched.

- The way a person holds her glass can say a lot: Stroking the glass gently can be a sign of interest, whereas quick tapping can be a sign of boredom.

- If you notice that someone is drinking her drink more quickly than usual, it could mean she is trying to finish her drink so she can leave. It can also signify nervousness.

124

opposed to what signs are warning of boredom or disinterest is key. Being fully cognizant and aware is crucial: Are you talking to someone who keeps stepping back as you step forward? Or are you engaged in conversation with someone who keeps seductively stroking the glass in her hand and stepping closer to you?

Although men sometimes boast of "taking charge" and approaching women, they are often unknowingly acting on signs, such as smiles and self-touching, that the woman has been exhibiting.

Know When to Back Off

- Crossed arms and legs, no eye contact, or a stance leaning toward another individual most likely mean a person isn't interested.

- If you notice someone stepping back each time you step forward, she is not comfortable with lessening the space between you.

- If you talk to someone whose eyes are wandering, she is not interested in the current conversation. End the encounter first and avoid rejection.

- "No" does indeed mean "no," and it is better to cut your losses and move on than to appear desperate.

Send Out Signals

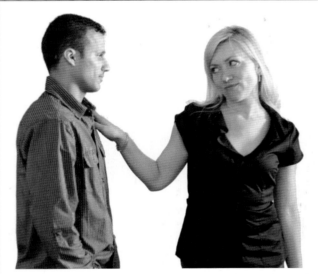

- Use the skills you've learned in earlier sections: You know that standing tall with a welcoming smile is inviting initial contact and conversation.

- Conversely, if you are trying to avoid an interaction, you know that crossed arms and averted eye contact signify a lack of interest.

- Use the cramped space of the bar to your advantage; this is a great space to test your boundaries with light touches on the arm to see how the other reacts.

125

SLEEPING SIGNALS

Are you a football or a spoon? The way you sleep can tell a lot about your romantic life

Sleeping next to each other can be one of the most intimate acts two people continuously make. Although much is written and discussed about physical acts in the bedroom, much less is said about the actual sleeping! Looking at how two people sleep can tell a lot about underlying problems and strengths in their relationship.

The spoon, football, and tetherball are some common couple sleeping positions, but many more exist, and a little reflecting and analyzing can give you much insight on the latent meaning of these sleeping styles.

The average person sleeps for one-third of his lifetime, so getting to know the meaning of sleeping positions is quite

Side Man

- The spooning position, with "big spoon" cupping "little spoon," is typical of couples in traditional relationships who like to follow norms of gender roles.

- Football position, facing each other with only one foot touching, is typical of modern, secure couples.

- Log position, lying on the side with arms flat against the body, can indicate a trusting but also gullible nature.

- Lying on your side can reduce sciatic pressure and is recommended for people with bad backs and pregnant women.

Back In

- Sleeping on your back with pillows underneath your knees to elevate your legs can be a comfortable way to take the pressure off your sciatica.

- Tetherball position (one person lying on his back with one arm touching the other person) can signify

independence in the relationship.

- Women in some cultures espouse sleeping on the back as a beauty trick to ward off wrinkles.

126

important! If you find that you are waking tense and not refreshed, a change in sleeping style may affect the quality of your sleep. Sleep positions can also be related to personality characteristics, as research by U.K. sleep specialist Chris Idzikowski found. The research described the personality meaning of different sleeping positions, such as lying in the fetus position (strong on the outside, sensitive on the inside, much more common in women) and lying with arms outstretched on the side (can be suspicious of others and stubborn to change after a decision has been made).

Face Plant

- Sleeping on your stomach is discouraged because it places excess pressure on the lower back.

- On the flip side, Dr. Yasuharu Tabara of Japan found that people who sleep on their stomachs may have lower nighttime blood pressure.

- Freefall position, lying flat on the stomach with hands wrapped around the pillow, can be a mark of anxiety-prone individuals who do not do well with criticism.

The Flailer

- The cliff-hanger position, on opposite sides of the bed, can be the beginning of distance/unresolved problems ... or just the result of different sleep schedules.

- Moving around in your sleep can be severely uncomfortable; one particular sleep problem is restless leg syndrome (RLS), which involves strange lower leg sensations and can disrupt normal sleep.

- Sleep positions are fairly stable and difficult to change, with less than 10 percent of individuals commenting that they change sleeping positions night to night.

ABOUT TO GET DUMPED

The body language-savvy person knows which signs can indicate romantic trouble

Just as it is important to know what signs to look for to determine if someone is interested in you, it is equally important to be aware of signs that indicate your partner may be losing interest. Although, as is true with all body language, there is no exact formula (your partner's eyes may be wandering simply because she is looking for a restroom!), it can be

extremely useful to make a mental note of body language cues that can signify waning interest.

The body language-savvy dater knows to be aware of certain signs while taking contextual and situational cues into account as well and making rational analyses of the romantic situation.

A romantic partner about to drift away will give off certain

Bad Romance

- If someone is facing you, but his legs and torso are pointed elsewhere, his attention is wherever his legs are pointed toward.

- Ambiguous emotions are often depicted by momentary facial tensing and movements that an individual may not even be aware of.

- Touching the neck, ear, or nose while telling a story can indicate that a lie is being told.

- Someone who increases the physical space from you is often also trying to decrease the emotional closeness you share.

Already Gone

- Body language expert Joe Navarro states that couples in troubled relationships use only their fingertips to touch each other.

- Exposure of the belly is reserved only for those we feel comfortable around (Navarro calls this "ventral fronting").

- If someone's gaze continuously wanders elsewhere, this can be a sign you are boring him and not holding his interest any longer.

- Look at pictures of divorced couples just prior to their breakup to see if you can find body language that foreboded their split.

body signals that can be decoded to convey insincerity. These range from fake smiles to increased lower body movements, particularly positioned away from you and toward an exit or other person.

Changes in standard body language are also noteworthy and should be assessed. For example, a partner who always provided warm embraces but has recently switched to tense pats on the back may be trying to communicate a loss of interest. Knowing what to look for is key: Disingenuous or cold body language could signify an impending breakup.

. . . . RED ● LIGHT . . . .

How much space your partner leaves between the two of you can be a good indicator of his or her comfort. If you notice that your partner leans back or moves to increase the distance between you, it probably isn't an accident—don't just keep pushing! Be aware of the message that he or she is trying to send.

DATING & MATING

Slammed Window

- "Windows," such as the eyes, palms, and neck, are sites of vulnerability and will be closed off around those with whom you are uncomfortable.

- Palm-to-palm touching can be a very intimate act, and couples on the verge of a breakup may find it difficult to do this.

- Having your palms or neck touched can be uncomfortable when done by someone you are losing feelings for.

- Conflicting emotions are often evident in the eyes.

Look for Insincerity in the Smile

- A Duchenne smile, or "real" smile, is one that involves stretching the mouth and eyes (that is, crow's-feet), whereas a fake smile involves stretching only the mouth.

- A real smile is unconscious, whereas a fake smile is voluntary and produced in the cerebral cortex.

- It is quite difficult to fake a genuine smile.

- In the animal kingdom, smiling is a sign of submission. Likewise, humans save their genuine smiles for those they are comfortable being vulnerable around.

OFFICE ROMANCE

The office is a particularly tricky arena to navigate in terms of romantic body language

Things can get tricky in an office romance because there is a fine line between conveying interest and stepping over the boundaries of appropriateness in the workplace. Workplaces have vastly different cultures, and keep in mind that many places of business still frown upon office romances. That said, there are ways to show interest without causing a Human Resources scandal. The rules of boundaries and space are especially important in the office setting. Although you can make yourself feel better after an awkward bar encounter by telling yourself, "I'll never see him again," you will be working alongside your work colleagues for as long as you hold your job, so the stakes are much higher.

Unmasked

- Being on elevators and public transit often makes people stand closer to others than space norms would dictate.

- It is standard to wear an expressionless "mask" in these situations to counter the space intrusion.

- To stand out from the masked masses, try engaging in a relaxed stance with a friendly expression and a slight smile.

- People are especially wary of others encroaching on their space in these tight situations—this is not the place to make a first move!

Sexy Space

- It is hard to exude confidence in a cluttered space; keep your work environment neat.

- A neat desk gives more space for open body language such as relaxed leaning and room to move around.

- Tailor your space as best you can to allow you to be at ease.

- Although touching a coworker may be off limits, touching the desk is not! Use the desk to rest your hand on to be conservatively suggestive.

Learn to really understand personal space norms and be careful not to encroach; keep in mind that whereas personal distance norms are around 2 feet, social distance norms (which are appropriate for the workplace) can range from 4 to 12 feet. If you do start a relationship with a colleague, it will most likely be necessary to engage in different distance norms depending on your environment (whether you are going out on a date or working together in the office). It's a good idea to be familiar with your company's policies on intraoffice dating before sending out your attraction signals.

······· YELLOW ● LIGHT ·······

It may be a wiser decision to save flirtation for an out-of-the-office rendezvous. Your colleagues work with you daily and most likely recognize your habits. Although you may think your flirtatious body language toward one person in particular is unnoticed by the rest of your colleagues, you are probably wrong. It is wiser to keep your love life under check while in the office.

Use Your Voice

- Because the office offers fewer opportunities for touching, use your voice as an extension of your body to show your confidence.

- An attractive voice is one that is not too loud or shrill and avoids nervous laughter.

- A 2009 article in the *Journal of Business Communications* found that laughter can be used to reduce tension and create a positive work environment.

Maintain Posture

- Don't let a desk job cramp your style, even when sitting and typing. Sit straight with back parallel to chair; it gives off a confident vibe and is better for your back.

- Sitting too close to your desk can make you appear closed off; leave some space.

- Your index finger resting on your cheek can indicate reflection, whereas your face being held up by your entire hand can convey boredom.

- Crossed arms and legs can make you appear closed off; try to maintain an open posture.

THE APPROACH

A first impression is long lasting and can make or break a budding romance

Dr. Monica Moore conducted research on singles looking to find dates and found that the more signals a single gives off, the more responses the single is likely to get. In other words, the single giving off confident smiles is more likely to get approached than his or her aloof counterpart.

It is increasingly standard that both men and women can make the initial approach; women need not feel as though they must wait for a man to approach them before they can begin conversing with him. Regardless of who makes the first move, the first impression is an important one.

Much research has been done on the first impression, and psychological research shows that people tend to have

For Him: Side Swoop

- Men feel less invaded when approached from the side.

- A man's dominant side, usually his right side but the left side for lefties, is the most comfortable side on which to approach him.

- Movements that are too quick, jumpy, or twitchy can make others nervous; try to make your approach as smooth as possible.

- Men interpret flirting signals more slowly than women do, so flirting signals may need to be repeated two to three times before they are picked up.

For Her: Front Approach

- Women prefer friendly approaches from the front.

- No one, and this is especially true of women, likes to be startled. A sneak-up from the back is not suave; it is alarming!

- People have different comfortable "private zones" and will move away to maintain this distance if they feel it is being crowded.

- There is a difference between confidence and aggressiveness: Save the touching for after a comfortable rapport has developed.

"confirmatory biases," which lead them to focus on information that confirms their initial hypothesis and to misinterpret information that could refute earlier beliefs. This means that your first impression will be long lasting and difficult to change later.

Take the other person's comfort level into account when planning your first approach. People don't like to feel bombarded or crowded—the more natural and organic you approach seems, the better!

Access Denied

- People can find it intimidating to approach you if you are in a crowd—if you want to be approached leave room for an entry.

- Take the group's positioning into account: A tightly closed circle may not want any interruptions, whereas a v-shaped duo may be open to a third party.

- Don't let crossed arms or legs be an automatic write-off: Some people cross limbs when nervous.

- Try a friendly smile prior to your approach. If it is returned, it can be the reassurance you need.

Access Allowed

- Note the differences in body language between this image and the prior image.

- When legs are pointing toward an open space or crowd of people, this sends an inviting message to potential "approachers."

- Avoid locking gazes for too long, which can be uncomfortable, or averting eye contact too quickly, which can be interpreted as nervous flirting—try to keep all motions smooth and confident.

- Crossed arms act as a barrier; keep arms uncrossed.

OFFICE SETUP
Your office space can act as an extension of your body communication

With increasingly hectic work schedules, it is quite common for adults to spend more waking hours in their work environments than in their homes. Still, although much thought goes into decorating one's home, less thought typically goes into decorating one's office.

Desks and cubicles may not be the first things that pop into your mind when you think of body language, but you can, in fact, use your office surroundings as a prop to enhance the image you are trying to portray. For example, a boss who wants to maintain an aura of authoritativeness and distance from employees can position the office desk so that it literally acts as a barrier designating a hierarchical separation.

Don't Get Caught Off Guard

- A desk facing the door allows full sight of what's going on outside the office.

- If you are in a separate office, and your back is away from the main door entrance, or the door is always closed, it is more difficult to develop a working rapport with your colleagues. The man in the image stays visible to the office.

- The more we are exposed to something, the more we like it—stay in full view of your colleagues!

- Get to know your space and be familiar with what is visible from different angles.

King of the Castle

- Seniority correlates with space; bigger spaces usually mean bigger paychecks and flashier titles.

- The boss never sits with her back to the door: A good boss positions her desk so that she is aware of everything going on outside and cannot be snuck up on.

- When asked to draw an ideal workspace, superiors are more likely to sketch an office separate from their subordinates.

- Awards and expensive art work all act as status symbols, which members of upper management use to highlight their status.

134

Psychologist Meredith M. Wells studied the relationship between office personalization and employee/organization well-being and found a positive correlation between a company's policy on personalization of the office space (for example, employees allowed to put pictures on their desks) and the overall well-being of the organization.

Wells also found a gender difference in that office personalization may have a greater impact on the well-being of women than on men. Office clutter has also been tied to higher levels of work-related stress.

Ergonomics is the science of ensuring that the workplace and job are tailored to fit the needs of the worker and is devoted to understanding how workspace can be tailored to avoid work-related injuries such as carpal tunnel syndrome.

Building a Fortress

- Plants, picture frames, and other objects are often used in smaller settings as a barrier to protect what little space is there.

- Personalized touches allow employees to maintain a degree of identity and uniqueness in the workplace.

- If your desk is too sequestered with high plants and shelves, colleagues walking by may feel less comfortable engaging in spontaneous dialogue with you.

Comfort Levels

- How often do you want people in your office? Having a comfortable spare chair in your office says to colleagues that you are interested in dialogue and collaboration.

- Candies on a desk can be an inviting conversation starter and a good excuse for others to stop at your desk.

- A sparse office with a big desk separating the center of the room can be intimidating.

- If your current office setup doesn't make you feel productive and comfortable, change it!

135

BOARDROOM

Circular or rectangular? The shape of your boardroom table can have important implications

Picking the right shape for your office board table is more than an aesthetic matter. Different boardroom table shapes are connected to different meanings about the seriousness of the meeting, the level of collaboration expected from employees, and hierarchical designations.

Body language authors Allen and Barbara Pease note that the person sitting to your right is usually a collaborative partner rather than an adversary. An interesting reasoning behind that is that the person to your right was historically less likely to stab you because this would mean he would use his left hand, which is the less-dominant hand in the majority of people. This highlights the importance of unconscious

KNACK BODY LANGUAGE

Rectangular Desk

- A rectangular desk shape signals authority and power.

- A rectangle has a clear head of the table and is thus ideal for when it is important to establish a hierarchy.

- This shape is used for formal meetings and is the most commonly seen in boardrooms.

- The person at the head farthest from the door is the one sitting in the "power seat."

Circular Desk

- A circular desk signals equality and lack of a hierarchical structure.

- This shape invites contribution and openness because there is no clear head, so employees of all levels feel comfortable to contribute their ideas.

- It is less popular than a rectangular desk but is becoming more common even in formal office settings.

- Circular desks seem to be more common in companies with female heads.

factors underlying the feelings and associations we make with different office setups and boardroom styles. We may not consciously know or acknowledge that we associate circles with collaboration and rectangles with hierarchy, but these associations do exist and can color the way we view office events and meetings. Make a mental note of different meeting types and the boardrooms in which they are held and see how your knowledge of the associations we make with different shapes and structures plays out.

Power Positions

- The two small widths of a rectangular table are the two power positions.

- The person sitting to the right of the head of the table farthest from the door is the second in command.

- With the advent of technological presentations, the presenter is typically in the "power seat" regardless of hierarchy.

- Even when strangers matched for socioeconomic class sit at a rectangular table, they are more likely to choose the person sitting in the "power seat" as their group leader.

Right-hand Woman

- The person who takes the seat to your right is most likely to be your supporter and open to collaboration.

- If you know in advance you want to develop a working relationship with someone, try to get a seat next to her at meetings, particularly on her right side.

- Meetings are a good place to begin working relationships because people go into meetings more ready to listen and cooperate.

- Norms about space are sometimes eased in board meetings because chairs are already provided and appropriately spaced.

WORKING RELATIONS

Power relations are at play in many of the day-to-day routines in your office

Try to notice the way people fill in empty rows in a theater or chairs at an open table. Unspoken norms dictate how we choose open seats, and people become uncomfortable when we act outside the boundaries of these norms. If you are one of the first to enter a meeting room with hundreds of empty chairs, for example, and a stranger who enters next takes a seat right next to you rather than taking one of the many empty spaces, you may find this a bit odd. Choosing seats is one of the areas where space and boundaries are particularly important.

Power relations are also at play with different seating choices. Whether you are conscious of it or not, choosing a

KNACK BODY LANGUAGE

Friendly Corners

- Sitting at the corners of a table promotes friendliness because there is no barrier separating you from your neighbor.

- If you are trying to placate a disgruntled colleague, try taking the corner seat across from him to signify your desire for better relations.

- Even if you are a touchy person by nature, your colleague may have different comfort zones than you do . . .

- . . . so don't allow your friendly seating position to make you act in unprofessional ways.

Side by Side

- Taking the seat next to a person, even though other chairs are available, signals openness to engage and cooperate.

- If the chair setup is such that you feel too close, feel free to adjust your chair position to maintain a comfortable space.

- Beware: It is easy for speakers to focus all their attention on those in front of them.

- If you take a seat next to someone you do not know very well in an office setting, it is appropriate to introduce yourself.

particular seat can prime a sense of cooperation or competitiveness in the person sitting next to or across from you.

Again, these norms are largely unspoken and taken for granted, but people may react negatively if the norms are violated. For example, your boss may not be pleased if you jump in and take the seat at the head of the table before he or she gets into the room. Although the seat may not be explicitly marked "for the most powerful person in here," that is exactly what is assumed about that particular position.

Showdown

- Taking the seat opposite a seated person (at table length) indicates competitiveness.

- Seats across from each other have a barrier separating the two parties, and this barrier can promote negative energy.

- You may find it difficult to speak to the person across from you if you are seated at a wide table, so plan accordingly.

- Being opposite someone primes feelings of Western-type showdowns, which may automatically prime competitive disagreement.

Top Dogs

- Taking the seat opposite a seated person (at table width) is the ultimate competition position.

- The two parties at the widths of a rectangle have the longest possible barrier separating them.

- This is a position in which power plays are in full effect.

- Be warned that the large distance between the two power seats can promote a shouting match to get voices heard.

139

WORKING RELATIONS (CONT.)
Knowing the social norms at your office will allow you to engage in impression management

Social norms are defined by sociologists as the behavioral expectations that a particular group holds about its members. Being familiar with a culture's or organization's social norms is important for "impression management" or the regulation of your nonverbal behavior in order to control the impressions that others make of you.

In the working environment, an example of impression management can be having a desk stacked with papers and making very little conversation with others in an environment that is highly competitive. Another example is commonly given by young professionals or academics who admit to unnecessarily wearing glasses, dying their hair prematurely gray, and taking

KNACK BODY LANGUAGE

I Sit, You Stand

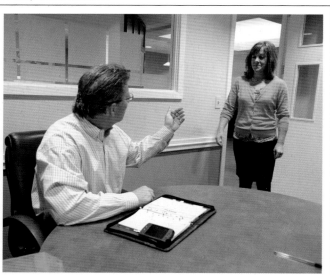

Independent Minded

- Staying seated when someone enters the office indicates you are in a position of power.

- It is considered rude in many cultures not to get up when someone enters the room for the first time.

- Notice that people are used to standing when people in power positions, such as clergy or judges, enter a room.

- Staying seated when everyone else is standing, unless you have a physical or health problem that prevents you from doing so, can be considered a form of protest.

- Sitting at the diagonals of a rectangular table indicates that you want to be left alone.

- If you are busy or do not want to engage in conversation with someone, take this seat.

- Many people take this posi-
tion out of shyness without realizing that it can shut them out of a conversation.

- As communal dining tables become popular, notice that Americans will take this seat if a stranger is the only other person sitting to maintain boundaries in an atypical dining situation.

on mannerisms associated with older age, such as sitting with arms in the steeple position, in order to make up for their lack in age with prominent displays of wisdom and authority.

It is important to be familiar with the working culture of your organization in order to act in appropriate ways to reach your career goals. Although coming into work wearing flip-flops and hopping onto your colleague's desk in order to have a conversation may be acceptable in a laidback or creativity-oriented environment, it will be decidedly less so in a traditionally professional workplace in which clients are coming and going.

Many bookstores now have "intro to culture" books that allow you to familiarize yourself with the basic norms in a culture to prevent you from putting yourself in an awkward situation. You will encounter differing business cultures not only on trips abroad but also in a diverse workplace.

Triangle of Trust

- Opening the angle from a straight line to a triangle lets a third party enter comfortably into the conversation.

- People are reluctant to enter into groups where members are tightly closed in.

- If you are talking in a pair, and a third party enters, taking a step back to form a triangle creates an automatic inclusion point.

- This is the better way to enter into the conversation of a duo than trying to squeeze in between the speaking parties.

A Leg Up

- Perching legs on a desk is the ultimate display of ownership and power; this is clear "alpha" behavior.

- Putting legs up on a table is not appropriate in most settings, and it can convey a sense of disrespect.

- Placing a leg up or sit-

ting with your legs tucked underneath your bottom is especially not appropriate if a superior is in the room.

- Having your legs up when an elder enters the room is the ultimate sign of disrespect in many cultures and can be taken as a direct insult.

DINNER PARTY
The formality of the dinner largely dictates seating arrangements

When thinking of proper dinner party etiquette, many are reminded of the film *Pretty Woman*, in which Julia Roberts's character is taught by a hotel manager how to use the confusing array of utensils, cups, and plates she will be faced with at an impending dinner party. Indeed, dinner etiquette can be a challenge for even the most cultured and educated of dinner guests.

Dinner party etiquette is an area largely influenced by culture; it is difficult to provide very many universal norms that are accepted regardless of cultural context. For example, whereas in many regions in the world dining is a social affair where loud conversations are standard even at quite formal events, dining etiquette in a Japanese context usually calls for minimal conversation. The animated exchanges typical of Turkish or Italian dining contexts are rarely considered appropriate at a formal Japanese dinner table.

It's in the Shape

- Egalitarian families in which equal gender roles are promoted tend to have circular tables for family dining.

- Traditional families with a clear head of the family are more likely to have a rectangular dining table.

- Square tables are less common in homes for dinner but more common in restaurants.

- Some families are used to sitting in the same position every night. If you are a guest, it is polite to ask if you should take any specific seat.

Dinner Is Served

- Buffets, in which all guests can serve themselves, are usually associated with more relaxed settings.

- Some people mistakenly consider buffets as "free for alls" where cutting in front of the line and grabbing at food are okay. They are not!

- Sit-down dinners are associated with more formal settings.

- The choice of buffet or sit-down can be largely cultural; buffets are more common in Middle Eastern and Asian contexts, with sit-down dinners in Italian and French contexts.

The seating arrangements typical of American dinner parties can vary depending on the formality of the event. More formal events, such as weddings, usually offer guests specific seating assignments. Whereas it was common up until the 1950s for the dinner hostess to tell her guests where to take a seat in even more laidback dining functions, this is no longer considered standard.

················· RED ● LIGHT ··············

The concepts discussed below are ones typical of American dining contexts and should not be taken as universal norms. Try searching travel guide books or make a quick Internet search to determine any norms specific to the region you are visiting. See Chapter 17 to learn more specifics.

Method to the Madness

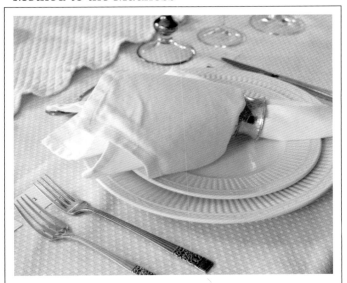

- When multiple courses are served, go from outward inward if in doubt of when to use what piece of cutlery.

- When you have finished eating, knife and fork should be placed in the center of the plate, lined up.

- At private dinner parties, the start of the meal is signaled by the host unfolding his napkin and placing it in his lap.

- It is polite to make short conversation with those seated next to you rather than to eat in silence the entirety of your meal.

Where to Sit

Ms. Linda Powell

- Let the host lead the seating—she may have seating cards, point you to a seat, or tell you to choose your own.

- Traditionally a female guest of honor sits to the right of the host, and a male guest of honor sits to the left of the hostess.

- If you choose to have seating cards, choose seating arrangements carefully to promote conversation and compatibility.

- If keeping with tradition, it is polite for men to rise when a woman leaves the table, sit, and then rise again when she returns.

CONE OF LEARNING
Choosing the right seat in the classroom isn't about just comfort; it may help your grade!

Classroom structure can vary from intimate seminars made up of a small number of students and an instructor nestled around a small table to massive auditoriums of hundreds of students, many of whom will never even say "Hello" to the professor teaching the class. With the prevalence of online and distance learning, classroom structure is shifting to even more independent enterprises.

Because classroom instruction, particularly at the college and graduate school levels, can be incredibly costly and time consuming, it is a good idea to familiarize oneself with the correlation between different seating locations and learning. Knowing this information, students can take their own needs

Cherry on Top

- There is typically a cone-shaped "learning zone" where those at the round top of the cone near the speaker retain and participate the most.

- Sitting at the front of the class "cone" lends itself to better learning and participation.

- One study found that students seated in the back and in corners farthest from the center had poorer self-concept and self-esteem.

Avoid the Corners

- Students sitting in back and far sides of classrooms learn and participate less than those in the front.

- If seating is open, try to sit inside the cone for optimal learning; otherwise, be aware that you will need to work extra hard to focus.

- The classroom stereotype is that those sitting in the back are the "snoozers."

- Students sitting in lecture hall balconies or in the far back of the room can be in embarrassing positions when caught reading a newspaper or sleeping midlecture.

into consideration and sit accordingly if free seating is permitted. Instructors can also use this information to pay closer attention to areas of the classroom known as "fall-off" areas where attention spans seem to drop off at a quicker rate.

Confident body positions, such as the steeple hand position or strong legs with a slight bend at the knee and a straight back, are important for both the instructor and the students. In both cases being prepared before the class (that is, students reading the material and the instructor prepping the lesson) will give them a better shot at conveying confident body language.

ZOOM

Looking attentively or nodding and smiling at appropriate times can be good positive reinforcement for a speaker to continue to look in your direction and keep you engaged. While listening to a speaker, look at him rather than keep your gaze to your lap or in other places.

Lucky Horseshoe

- The horseshoe (sometimes called the "U shape") classroom setup is becoming popular in many class and seminar settings.

- Less-traditional modes of classroom setup can promote communication and involvement of students.

- This setup allows students to make eye contact with more of their peers and may serve to keep students engaged because they are being policed by their peers.

- Ask to be seated somewhere else or to shift your desk if you have problems seeing or hearing the lesson.

Be Seen

- Educators need to walk around the room to engage students and avoid falling out of eyesight.

- The horseshoe setup can allow the educator to walk closely by all of the students without having his back turned for too long.

- An audience can detect fear, and it is up to the speaker to convey confidence via strong hand positions and an authoritative gait or stance.

- Use prewritten projections or slides to avoid having your back turned for long periods of time.

EYEGLASSES

What helps you see may be changing the way you're seen

If you've worn eyeglasses for much of your life, you are probably comfortable with the idea of your glasses being an extension of your body. Just try to imagine all the times you touch your glasses over the course of a day. You probably don't even notice when you take them off, hold them in your hand, or gesture with them. As with all props, using glasses can be a double-edged sword. Used properly, they can help enhance your image. Used improperly, they can hurt it.

Whether you're talking to your coworker, boss, or employee, it's important to be aware of both how you use your glasses and how others use theirs. For example, are you constantly adjusting them or pushing them up the bridge of your nose? Are you whipping them off when you're surprised or make an important point? Do you hold them in your hand and use them to point? Does your boss peer at you over his glasses? Does he take them off to clean them when you're explaining

Fidgeting with Your Eyeglasses

- If you wear glasses, make sure you're not constantly fidgeting with them.

- Continually adjusting eyeglasses can signal nervousness.

- If someone else is pushing his eyeglasses up and down the bridge of his nose, it could mean he disagrees with you.

- Glancing down and pushing your glasses up can appear similar to a gesture of shame (head down, touching brow), so make sure you're not sending the wrong signal.

Gesturing with Your Eyeglasses

- If your boss removes his glasses, it could mean he wants to hear more.

- Shedding those specs could also mean your boss is unhappy with the current state of affairs.

- Glasses can replace an index finger and be used to direct attention.

- If you need a moment to think or consider something before speaking, removing your glasses can provide you with time to do so without making the interaction awkward.

something? For you to be understood completely when you're conveying your message, your body language must match your words. Your eyeglasses help you see more clearly, but they can also help the real you be seen more clearly by others and help your message to be heard and understood as well.

Peering over the Rims of Your Eyeglasses

- When you look at someone with your chin down and your head tilted forward, you're literally looking down on her or him.

- Peering over your glasses has the same effect and can make you look superior.

- If someone else peers over his glasses at you, he could signal that he is scrutinizing you.

- Peering over your glasses in this way can make you appear older to others.

Touching Your Glasses to Your Mouth

- Anytime your hand lightly touches your face while someone else is talking, you're sending the signal that you're listening and thinking critically.

- This gesture can be enhanced by putting the end of one of your eyeglass arms into your mouth.

- Use this gesture when you want to indicate to the speaker that you're interested in what he's saying.

- To enhance your appearance of engagement, tilt your head slightly with the arm of your glasses in your mouth.

PROPS

PENS & NOTECARDS

Be mindful of your presentation props, and they will help relate your point rather than hinder it

If you work in an office, have a lot of meetings, and give presentations, you probably spend much of your time with pens and notecards in your hands. Pens are a necessary part of any job, and your mastery of them as a body language prop is an almost equally indispensable tool. Do you click your pen incessantly, bothering those around you? Do you use your pen to point? Do you touch it lightly to the corner of your mouth or chew on it? These are all important behaviors to be aware of whether you're listening to a presentation or giving one yourself.

If giving a presentation, you must be mindful of how you use notecards. Notecards are great reminders, but you shouldn't

Clicking Your Pen

- Not only is clicking a pen distracting to others, but also it sends the signal that you're distracted.

- Incessant clicking can also signal nervousness and anxiety.

- To prevent yourself from clicking a pen, hold the pen in between your thumb and index finger instead of in your fist.

- If you find yourself unable to kick the clicking habit, switch to a pen with no click top.

Holding Your Notecards

- The distance of your notecards to your body indicates how comfortable you are.

- Hugging the notecards close to your chest sends the message that you're extremely uncomfortable.

- You should use notecards only as reminders and never read directly from them.

- Be mindful that notecards create a barrier between yourself and your audience and keep them to the side as much as possible.

rely on them exclusively. Not only does the act of reading from notecards alienate you from the audience, but also the notecards themselves create a barrier between yourself and your audience. It's best to keep notecards to the side for the bulk of the presentation to ensure your body language remains open, confident, and engaging. This helps you build and maintain rapport with members of the audience, ensuring they're attentive and receptive to your message. If you want your meeting to impress your boss and engross your coworkers, make sure you use all the tools at your disposal.

ZOOM

When we get nervous or anxious, we often perform self-touch gestures as a way to calm ourselves. Picking at your cuticles, wringing your hands, and cracking your knuckles are all examples of self-touch gestures. Because a pen can often feel like an extension of your body, clicking, or flexing, a pen can be interpreted as a self-touch gesture and can make you appear nervous.

Touching Your Pen to Your Face

- A pen lightly touching the corner of your mouth can signal that you're deep in thought.

- Be careful not to overdo it, or else you can appear to be hushing yourself.

- A pen over the center of your lips in this "hushed" position can be interpreted by others that you're holding something back.

- Avoid supporting your head with your hand while touching a pen to your mouth. This posture can send the signal that you're bored or uninterested.

Taking Notes

- Readying your pen for writing makes you look eager and attentive.

- To look even more engaged, tilt your head a bit to signal that you're listening.

- Nodding slightly every few moments while writing indicates a positive reaction to the speaker.

- Remember not to break eye contact for too long while you write. Write a few sentences and glance up so the speaker knows you're invested and not distracted.

PROPS

BEER BOTTLES & WINE GLASSES

Whether you are drinking cocktails or water, these are always some great props to employ

Most people enjoy having a drink or two when they're out with friends or coworkers. For some people drinking and socializing are a relaxing experience in which they can blow off some steam. For others social drinking can be nerve wracking, and plenty of questions may race through their mind. What should you do with your hands? Where should you position yourself when talking with a group? How should you hold your drink?

If you're out at a bar drinking, cans, bottles, and glasses provide natural props. As with all props, however, the trick is to use them correctly. For example, others' perceptions of you will differ dramatically depending on whether you use your

Sipping Your Drink

- Be wary of taking long, constant sips from your drink because doing so can make you look nervous.

- If you take long sips, not only will you end up drinking more, but also you won't be able to have a conversation with others when a glass is blocking your mouth.

- Position yourself toward the middle of a group of people so you'll appear to be the center of attention.

- Being in the middle of a group can also make others more likely to engage you.

Holding Your Drink

- Never hold your drink with two hands in front of you.

- Holding your drink in front of your chest makes you look closed off.

- Hugging your drink closely to your body can send the message to those around you that you're uncomfortable in a social situation.

- When you block your chest with your drink, you look as though you don't want to be approached.

drink to close yourself off or use it to entice someone to talk to you. Although you may not always want to be approached when you're drinking, knowing the signals you're sending is essential to getting what you want.

More and more often, work carries over from business hours to happy hour, so it's important to bring your best body language from the office to the bar. Depending on the situation, you may want to appear professional, casual, comfortable, or confident. How you hold your drink and carry yourself can go a long way to accomplishing these goals.

Playing with the Rim of Your Glass

- Playing with the rim of your glass can be interpreted as flirting.

- When toying with the rim of your glass, don't do it too rapidly, or else you'll appear nervous.

- Practicing can make this gesture appear more natural.

- To enhance this flirtatious move, tilt your head down a bit and look forward or slightly upward.

Keeping Your Drink at Your Side

- When you hold your glass in front of your body, your arm creates a barrier between you and the person you're talking to.

- Creating a barrier in this way can block others from the conversation.

- Instead, holding your drink by your side creates the impression that you're open and willing to engage.

- When you're not taking a sip, hold your drink by your side to let others in and let your best body language shine.

PROPS

SMOKING
This is a new kind of smoke signal to use if you aren't stranded

In social situations many people enjoy drinking and smoking. Like drinking, smoking requires both the hands and the mouth. In fact, often people smoke during social activities simply because they don't know what else to do with their hands. Because your hands and face are busy, you may think you don't have to worry about body language and facial expressions when you're smoking, but that's not the case. With all social activities you must always be aware of what signals your body language, gestures, and facial expressions are sending to those around you.

When actors portray characters who smoke, they often use the act of smoking to add more depth to the character and make them seem more real. For example, when John Travolta played teen heartthrob Danny Zuko in the film *Grease*, he let a cigarette dangle effortlessly from his mouth. When he played an elite cyberterrorist in the film *Swordfish*, he smoked long,

Blowing Smoke Upward

- Blowing smoke upward and away from others can be interpreted as polite.

- It can also make you appear more confident.

- But be wary of your other body language signals

- because blowing smoke upward can also be interpreted as arrogant.

- If you blow smoke upward, make sure you're not breaking eye contact for too long during a conversation.

Ashtray Etiquette

- Leaving your cigarette burning in an ashtray can indicate that you're preoccupied.

- Forgetting about a cigarette and lighting another can be perceived by others as a sign of irresponsibility or distraction.

- Abruptly extinguishing your cigarettes can signal to others that you're anxious.

- Chain-smoking can also indicate nervousness.

thin cigars held with all four fingers. When he played rough-around-the-edges mob henchman Vincent Vega in the film *Pulp Fiction*, he smoked hand-rolled cigarettes held between his middle two knuckles. You can do the same thing using what you smoke, how you hold it, and how you smoke it. Although smoking is usually considered a vice, you can use these tips, tricks, and techniques to turn it into an advantage.

Blowing Smoke Downward

- Tilting your head downward and looking forward make your eyes appear narrower.

- This posture can make you appear more sinister and less trustworthy. Blowing smoke downward enhances this effect.

- Dropping your gaze while you blow smoke downward can indicate concern or anxiety.

- You may also be breaking eye contact when you blow smoke downward, appearing less engaged.

Blowing Smoke through Your Nostrils

- Blowing smoke through your nose makes your nostrils flare.

- This nostril flare can make you appear more aggressive.

- An angry facial expression can compound this effect.

- Blowing smoke through your nostrils while you're smiling and open can make you appear confident instead of aggressive.

PROPS

WOMEN VERSUS MEN

Is confidence the key or just good body language?

Because men and women carry themselves differently and are perceived differently, they often have different body language problems and solutions. These differences are more pronounced in social situations such as bars and singles clubs than they are in the workplace. Differences between men's and women's body language can become especially exaggerated when dating. Because of this fact, men and women can often employ different strategies when flirting.

For example, some women prefer to play the coy type, appearing more vulnerable. On the other hand, some men prefer to enhance their apparent power, authority, and success to attract others.

For both genders it's about appearing confident, open, and approachable. Men and women alike are attracted to confidence. If you appear open, you're more likely to be perceived as honest, trustworthy, and pleasant. If you want someone

Exposing Your Wrists

- If you're a woman, smoking allows you to easily expose your wrists.

- Exposing your wrists makes you appear more vulnerable and open.

- Wrist exposure can signal a willingness to engage.

- This vulnerability and openness can make you appear more attractive to men.

Covering Your Mouth

- Covering half your face restricts your ability to communicate nonverbally through facial expressions.

- Covering your mouth can indicate shyness or unwillingness to engage.

- Blocking your body in this way creates a barrier.

- This can send the signal that you're closed off or uninterested.

to notice and engage with you, you need to look like you're willing to be approached instead of closed off or shut down. You may feel anxious, nervous, distracted, or upset, but it's important not to appear that way to others. As with all body language, you must be aware of the signals you send as well as the signals others send. Social situations can make both women and men nervous, so developing good body language takes practice for everyone.

YELLOW ● LIGHT

Although covering your face with a menu like a geisha girl with a fan can make you look coy or coquettish, overdoing it can make you look like you're hiding, timid, or embarrassed. The more of you your date can see, the more information you're giving him or her. If you want to appear confident, open, and approachable, keep your face and body visible at all times.

Cigars

- Cigars are associated with a sense of superiority.

- Many people blow smoke upward when they smoke cigars, enhancing signals of superiority.

-

- The amount of time you leave a cigar label on indicates the level of desire you wish your status to be registered.

- For good body language, your comfort is key. Don't start smoking cigars if you don't enjoy the smell.

Loosening Up

- Loosening your tie can help expose your neck.

- An exposed neck can make you appear more comfortable and confident.

- Pulling at your tie can indicate discomfort and distress.

- Fidgeting with your tie knot can block your neck, making you appear anxious, upset, or uncomfortable.

PROPS

155

SALES

Body language plays a key role in distinguishing good salespeople from mediocre ones

"Sales are contingent upon the attitude of the salesman—not the attitude of the prospect." In this quote businessman and philanthropist W. Clement Stone describes one of the most basic tenets of sales. Though the client is the one with the money making the purchase, a well-trained and seasoned salesperson can very well turn the tables to lead the interaction and ultimately gain the upper hand.

The salesperson can be thought of as the ambassador for the product; his confidence allows the client to feel confident about the product. Unfortunately, salespeople often must compete with existing stereotypes of the "snake-oil salesperson" or charlatans who would trick unsuspecting customers

Maintain Open Body Language

- Eye contact, posture, and facial expression should be positive and inviting.

- Body language and the sales pitch should match, so if you are talking up the product, make sure your body is also alert and engaged.

- Crossed arms make you appear standoffish to the client, as if you may be hiding something.

- Smiling and nodding while listening to clients allow them to feel as though their opinions are valuable and being heard.

Cool as a Cucumber

- Ensure that the sales location is cool to avoid excessive sweating because it is associated with nervousness and anxiety.

- If you are perspiring, wear dark colors and excuse yourself if possible to freshen up.

- Although sweat on the body can be masked by clothing choices, beads of sweat on the forehead can be an obvious sign that the salesperson is anxious.

- A salesperson who is thirsty or hungry may be giving uncomfortable/impatient vibes.

into paying for useless products. Thus, the salesperson is in the delicate role of displaying enough confidence to relax the client about an impending purchase while not overdoing it. The salesperson must exude an attitude that says (1) I am confident in the product I am selling and (2) the product is so valuable to you that it really speaks for itself, and I am just an ambassador for this product. Thus, the main tasks for the salesperson are to gain the trust of the client (that is, build rapport) and establish the product as a valuable asset to the client (that is, by exuding self-confidence).

Touch of Confidence

- Touching and mirroring should be employed appropriately to develop a bond between salesperson and client.

- The intention of touching is to establish a familiar connection and develop a comfortable, friendly dialogue.

- Some clients, however, will not appreciate being touched according to their personal boundary norms.

- A salesperson should use only a light touch, such as a hand pausing for a moment on the client's arm, if he is 100 percent sure that the client will be receptive.

Show Interest

- Express interest in the subject by leaning forward and nodding at the appropriate moments.

- Distance between the salesperson and client is key: Too close could feel intrusive, whereas too far can come off as rude or distant.

- The steeple position shows interest and reflection by the salesperson and a potential interest to buy and weighing of the options by the client.

- Leaning to show interest is okay, but slouching so that your posture is more casual than your client's is not!

SELLING YOURSELF

MIRRORING
When it comes to building rapport, imitation done properly can be an invaluable bonding tool

Think about people with whom you feel a connection. Chances are that the feeling of connectedness is based on commonalities the two of you share. After all, people like people who are like themselves.

Although in some cases opposites attract, finding common ground is a quick and almost sure-fire way to establish rapport.

You may try to discover or call attention to some likenesses during the initial small talk in order to get the conversation flowing. Discussing similar backgrounds or a topic both parties are interested in and knowledgeable about will create a comfortable atmosphere, which is crucial to build rapport.

Along with commonalities in background or interests,

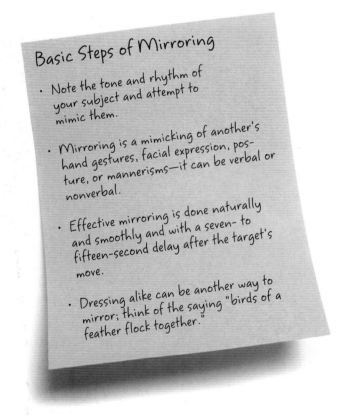

Basic Steps of Mirroring

- Note the tone and rhythm of your subject and attempt to mimic them.

- Mirroring is a mimicking of another's hand gestures, facial expression, posture, or mannerisms—it can be verbal or nonverbal.

- Effective mirroring is done naturally and smoothly and with a seven- to fifteen-second delay after the target's move.

- Dressing alike can be another way to mirror; think of the saying "birds of a feather flock together."

Line of Fire

- Interviewee sitting in line with the interviewer (that is, chairs are facing each other straight on).

- Sitting face to face allows you to see the other's facial expressions and match them as appropriate.

- Not mirroring at appropri-

ate times can make the conversation awkward. For example, it can be awkward if someone laughs, and you stare at him or her with a straight face.

- If you feel unsure of how to mirror, start with the basics, such as matching nods and smiles.

physically resembling your new acquaintance also serves to form an almost instant bond. Dressing alike or having similar hair styles could do the trick, but many times this is not an option. One physical strategy that anyone can use is called *mirroring*, by which you loosely imitate the other person's body language. When mirroring, remember to begin small (that is, match the strength of the handshake, return a smile, speak at the same rate) and progress to larger, more noticeable moves. When making these larger imitations, wait a few seconds so you do not make your efforts obvious.

Posture Rules

- Matching the posture of your target gives the feeling that you both have the same intentions.

- In general it is appropriate for the subordinate to mirror the superior.

- In business the interviewee should not have a more relaxed posture than the interviewer, and the seller should not have a more relaxed posture than the buyer.

Match the Hands

- A good mirroring strategy is to match your subject's hand positions, such as sitting with hands on a desk with fingers intertwined.

- Hand gestures are commonly used to emphasize a point, and mirroring appropriately can signal that you have the same goals in mind.

- Group mirrored hand gestures. For example, standing with hands clasped in front can convey unity and a united team.

- It can look fake, or even comical, to mirror unusual or highly emotion-laden hand motions.

159

TOUCHING

The sense of touch can be used in mirroring to both form bonds and assert dominance

The sense of touch has an important role in social bonding—the basic, primal necessity of touch can be seen from the grooming activities of various animals to the importance of the nurturing touch of a mother to the development of a child. In fact, psychologist Harry Harlow's famous "surrogate mother experiment" conducted with baby rhesus monkeys separated from their mothers showed that given the choice, the monkeys prefer spending their time with a fake monkey made out of a soft huggable fabric than with a monkey made out of wire (unhuggable) that provided food.

Touch is necessary in the normal development of a human child, and the absence of it can have truly devastating

Gaining the Upper Hand

- Touch between men is often a sign of superiority; if a man is touched by a subject, he can counter to reassert his own authority.

- Touch between women is often a sign of comforting or bonding; if a woman is touched, she can counter to show mutual rapport.

- Sudden, forceful touch is common in friendly settings and not appropriate in the workplace.

- It is generally more acceptable for two women who have just met to touch than it is for two men or a man and a woman.

Persuasive Touch

- Behavioral scientists Guéguen and Fischer-Lokou showed in a series of experiments that patrons are more likely to take the suggestion of their waiter if it is accompanied with a subtle touch on the arm.

- A brief touch can develop a bond between subjects and make them feel like they are on the same team.

- A touch that is too long or lingering, contrastingly, can feel threatening or bullying when accompanied by a suggestion.

consequences for the social development, and even health, of children. Even when we are adults, touch continues to hold an important role in the forming of social bonds and, when used appropriately, can help form or serve to cement feelings of closeness with others. Although touch can be a useful tool in facilitating bonding, in the age of sexual harassment laws and changing norms of what is appropriate professional touching, it is better to err on the side of caution and avoid touching those you have a professional relationship with.

ZOOM

Note that different cultures have different norms about what is appropriate touch, and Mediterranean and Latin cultures tend to be more open with touching and embracing than other cultures.

Friendly Pat on the Arm

- Touching the back of the arm or back usually indicates sympathy or friendship.

- Coupling an arm or back pat with a nod or smile further emphasizes the desire to bond.

- To comfort a friend who is emotional or distressed, grabbing one of his or her hands and holding it in both of yours can be a powerful comforting signal.

- It is more common for women to engage in softer, fluid pats, whereas men more often use quick, light pats on the arm or back.

Guiding Touch

- The back and the arm should also be the focus areas for physically guiding an individual.

- Pointing the way with an outstretched hand and open palm is more inviting than simply pointing.

- Touching to build rapport should feel natural. If you feel forced or awkward, it could be a sign that it is not appropriate to touch.

- Using a light touch on the back to guide a date to her seat is a common way for men to initiate touch in a natural way on a first date.

161

SELLING YOURSELF

PUBLIC SPEAKING
A successful speaker makes audience members feel the speaker is engaged and focused on them

Think back to the last time you were in the audience of a truly talented speaker. Although different speakers employ different styles—some are loud and flamboyant, whereas others are calm and poised—good public speakers all have one thing in common: the ability to make their audience feel special and engaged. They do this by building rapport with the audience.

Building rapport with an audience can be a daunting task for a public speaker; it can be hard enough to establish rapport when in close proximity with someone in a one-on-one conversation, let alone when surrounded by a mass of individuals all looking at you to entertain, educate, and engage them. A good speaker speaks with conviction, makes eye

The Right Way to Make Arm Gestures

- Gesture during your speech using the entirety of your arms because small hands-only gestures may be missed by those sitting farther away.

- Ensure that arm gestures are high enough to be seen but don't distract from your face.

- Be aware of your hands even when you're not directly gesturing—closed fists at your side can seem angry, and tapping fingers can make you look nervous.

- Overly choreographed hand and arm gestures can seem too theatrical; use smooth, casual gestures.

Behind a Wall

- If possible, avoid standing behind a podium because it can act as a barrier making your audience feel closed off.

- A podium can remind you to stand straight, so without one, remember to keep an upright posture with feet pointed toward the crowd.

- Feet should be not quite shoulder width apart, and legs should be slightly bent at the knee because locked knees can make you more likely to stumble.

- If a podium is needed, use open (palms out) gestures and walk in front of the barrier to answer questions.

contact with the audience throughout the presentation, stands in a comfortable stance, uses appropriate hand gestures that are not affected or distracting, and uses multimedia—if at all—as a tool rather than as a crutch.

Additionally, it is difficult for an audience to begin to develop a rapport with a speaker who displays incongruence because such incongruence can make the speaker seem fake and untrustworthy. For example, a speaker who says, "I am extremely excited to speak about . . ." but lacks excitement in facial gestures or tone of voice will quickly lose his audience.

PowerPoint Is Not Always Your Friend!

- Visual material should be aids, not the focus of the presentation, because such material can make an audience feel detached from the speaker. Minimize video clips, sounds, and fancy fonts.

- Use visual material as a top-level summary to guide the discussion, not as an exact transcript of your presentation.

- Practice using visual aids and props before the presentation so you don't lose connection with your audience by focusing your attention on getting faulty programs to work.

Gaze Wisely

- Employ the three-second rule and stare at a person in the audience for three seconds at a time—don't stare too long at a person or avert your gaze too quickly.

- Occasionally do a full scan of the audience to mix up your eye contact style.

- Try not to use notes because looking down to read them can bore the audience.

- Use eye contact as a tool to make individual members of the audience feel special and involved in your presentation.

SELLING YOURSELF

CHECKING YOUR OWN NORMS

Be aware of your "default" moves to match your body language to the needs of any situation

Although the universality of facial expressions has been discussed in previous chapters, and general rules and tactics for effective body language have been discussed throughout this book, this section discusses the unique gestures, facial expressions, stances, and voice tone we all bring into the nonverbal communication stage.

Being aware of these individual idiosyncrasies allows us to effectively tailor our body communication "norms" to fit a given situation. For example, if you know you are the type of person who tends to slouch, you can be aware of this and make an added effort to stand or sit straight in a situation where it is important to display your confidence, such as

Watch Yourself!

- Monitor your hand gestures during social interactions.

- Effective speakers use hand gestures to punctuate or add emphasis on their statements.

- Too few hand gestures can make you appear rigid

and bore your audience, whereas too many can be distracting.

- Watch clips of famous speeches or effective presentations to get an idea of how to effectively use hand gestures.

Don't Give Your Boredom Away

- Take note of any hand-to-face contact and relate it to the climate of your social conditions.

- Resting your head on your hands is a tell-tale sign that you are bored and can make it easier to doze off unwittingly.

- If you do need to rest your head, try using the steeple (head leaning on chin and index finger), which makes you look as though you are deep in thought.

- Touching your fingers to your mouth can made look unprofessional because it is a gesture made when lying.

when approaching your boss for a raise or finalizing a big deal with a client. People differ in the level to which they change verbal and nonverbal communication to match the situations they are in—those who tend to regulate their behaviors and constantly adjust them to match different situations and environments are called "high self-monitors," based on psychologist Mark Snyder's self-monitoring theory. In a pivotal experiment he found that university students at Stanford were rated higher than psychiatric patients but lower than professional actors in their level of self-monitoring.

Find Your Posture Equilibrium

- Develop a posture that is neutral and confident as second nature.

- Although you may have to consciously work at it in the beginning, good posture is a habit that can learned over time.

- Good posture—a straight back with feet facing forward—is a natural way to convey confidence.

- Good posture doesn't mean sitting straight as a board; you can lean forward to emphasize a point and use hand gestures to make your posture your own.

PROPped Up

- Consider props inherent in the social interaction as an independent component and treat them accordingly.

- Holding a glass in your hand can be a good use of your hands to hide any awkward fidgeting.

- Props should not, however, become a distraction—think of how annoying it is trying to listen to someone who keeps tapping his pen on the desk.

- Props can sometimes act as a barrier that prevents you from building rapport.

SELLING YOURSELF

THE FIRST IMPRESSION
"You never get a second chance to make a first impression" is trite but true

Caricaturists make a living by capturing a person's essence within a few moments. Many people shy away from these playful drawings because they are scared of what their first impression might reveal about them. You probably don't think of it much, but people are making snap judgments about you every day. This is especially true in the interviewing process. Before showing up at your next job or college admittance interview, think of how you are perceived at first glance. Are you sharply or sloppily dressed? Do you exude confidence or diffidence? Does it look as if you are well rested or as if you were up all night? All of these elements matter when aiming to make a great first impression.

Give Interviewer the Upper Hand

- Make the handshake strong by shaking web to web for two to three seconds, applying pressure similar to your interviewer's.

- The palm-up gesture during the handshake is considered submissive, as if you are saying, "You're the boss."

- Although your interviewer is not likely to be cognizant of your intentions with this move, he will still feel your conferral of power.

- Giving the upper hand is effective during an interview, but be careful in other situations when you want to be perceived as an equal.

Maintain Eye Contact

- Maintaining eye contact throughout the handshake shows mutual acknowledgment and sincerity.

- Proper eye contact is essential when establishing rapport.

- Shy people tend to give less eye contact and are sometimes perceived as untrustworthy.

- If you tend to shy away from full eye contact, concentrate on looking at the triangle region between the right eye, left eye, and the bridge of the nose. It will appear as if you are giving eye contact.

Much researching has been done on the importance of a first impression. Although most agree that this impossible-to-change judgment is made within the first two minutes of meeting a person, recent research shows that this figure is grossly overestimated. Although your interviewer is likely to sum you up during the entire interview process, the first impression occurs subconsciously in less than two seconds.

You should embrace the power of a first impression and ensure that your body language is helping you make an awesome one.

Maintain Good Posture

- Approach and shake hands with good posture. Good posture is comfortably upright, not so upright that you look militant and stiff.

- Upright posture conveys self-confidence as well as interest in your contact, whereas sloppy posture indicates indifference.

- While shaking hands, do not lean into or out of the shake. These leans could make you seem either too eager or standoffish.

- While shaking hands you may tilt your head, which appears friendly and open.

Bring in the Smile

- Wait until your interviewer says his or her name, then flash a smile that engages both the mouth and eyes.

- Scientific research has reliably distinguished between real and fake smiles. A genuine, "Duchenne" smile crinkles the outer corners of the eyes into crow's-feet.

- Most people can intuitively tell with relative accuracy whether a smile is genuine.

- Smiling while repeating the interviewer's first name is a good way to build rapport.

TAKING A SEAT

Do you put enough thought into your actions when told to "Please take a seat"?

Consider what was running through your head the first time you entered the high school cafeteria. Where should you sit? Who should you sit next to and across from? What do you do when you are done eating? You probably haven't thought much about strategic seating since those high school cafeteria days, but, as it turns out, where you place yourself relative to the interviewer and how you sit during an interview really do matter.

Incorrectly going about this simple step of taking a seat can create unwanted barriers or distance between you and the interviewer, make you appear insecure, or create a closed-off and uncomfortable atmosphere for both parties. Don't

Engage by Leaning Forward

- Position yourself slightly forward in your chair, maintaining upright posture with a slight lean.

- The upright posture conveys confidence, whereas the lean toward the interviewer conveys interest.

- Do not be afraid to change your posture when speaking versus listening or when something piques your interest.

- Your goal should be to appear comfortable while not too casual or relaxed, interested and actively listening while not too eager or tense.

Line Up

- Position yourself in line with the interviewer.

- Choose a seat opposite the interviewer, where your body is square with his or hers.

- Angle your body toward the interviewer instead of toward the door or a win-

- dow; the latter will make you appear anxious for an escape.

- If you notice the interviewer angle away from you suddenly, it could indicate a disagreement.

overlook it or underestimate its importance.

When you are welcomed into the interviewer's office, you are entering his personal space. Your entrance which may at first feel like an intrusion, is your first opportunity to prove that you belong there. If you use body language effectively and choose seating that makes both the interviewer and you feel at ease, it is only a matter of time until it will feel like you are a fit to be welcomed permanently into that world.

Avoid Crossed Arms and Legs

- Crossed arms or legs send the signal that one is closed off.

- While talking, use your hands to make purposeful gestures that match your words.

- While listening, rest your hands on the table or arm rests, never in your lap or where the interviewer can't see them.

- Sit with legs 6 to 12 inches apart (men) or together and to the side (women), being careful to not hide them under the chair.

Practice Active Listening

- While listening, tilt your head slightly and give the speaker eye contact.

- The tilt shows the speaker that you are respectfully listening while he or she speaks.

- Nod periodically to express agreement and under- standing. Nods should be slow and deliberate, not quick and choppy.

- If you are not in agreement with the speaker, wait until his or her thought is finished before resuming a level head while you express your opinion.

QUESTIONS & ANSWERS

You've tackled the intros and information phases; now it's time for two-player Q&A

"What are your salary requirements? Where do you see yourself in three years? Tell me about a time when you failed."

You may be tempted to breathe a sigh of relief and relax a little bit after the introductions and information sessions are over, and it is time for questions. After all, you have done your research and are prepared to answer whatever questions are thrown your way. You may even have some tricky questions up your sleeve for when the interviewer gives you the mic.

By this time you have probably become accustomed to your surroundings and can picture yourself working in a similar office across the hall. Although you have gotten through what may have been an uncomfortable beginning, it is still

Raise Your Voice

- During Q&A both what you say and how you say it are taken into consideration.

- A monotone voice is likely to lose the interviewer's attention. Regulate the loudness, inflection, and content of your words.

- Sit up straight. The strength of your voice comes from your lower rib cage, and slumped posture minimizes the amount of air that you can breathe in and out during speech.

- Inflect when you speak. Inflection is the alteration in pitch or tone. It is the color in your voice when you tell a story.

Pause Purposefully to Plan

- When presented with a tough question, take a brief moment to think about all the facts you want to include in your response.

- Having a well-thought-out response is always better than blurting out a scatterbrained answer to avoid silence.

- Touch your chin with your thumb and index finger or tilt your head to the side to let the interviewer know you are thinking during your silence.

- When you do answer, move your head back in a level position.

important to be aware of your body language for the remainder of the interview in order to maintain the open, natural, and comfortable atmosphere you worked to create.

During the question-and-answer phase, you are being evaluated on your two-way communication skills. Are you able to pose questions and listen actively by nodding and tilting your head as well as answer the interviewer's questions with confident and self-assured body language? Can you hold the interviewer's attention long enough to convince him or her that you are the right man or woman for the job?

Keep Your Chin Up

- Avoid looking down during the interview; looking down comes across as nervous, shy, and evasive.

- If you need to look down, look at something on the table, such as your own notes or the interviewer's papers.

- Doing this is especially important when answering a question; the voice tends to trail off when the speaker looks down.

- If you need to get something out of your bag during an interview, make sure you do not do this while speaking.

Occasionally Break Eye Contact

- In a professional setting, the appropriate length of time for continuous eye contact is about five seconds.

- Keep eye contact 60 to 80 percent of the time. To break eye contact, look to the right or left briefly but not at your lap or the ground.

- While listening, give about 80 percent eye contact; while speaking, stay at around 60 percent.

- Do not look at the interviewer's mouth; it is considered sexual, and the interviewer is likely to notice.

THINGS TO AVOID
Learn which body language moves are considered "taboo" and how to avoid them

Close your eyes and imagine the worst possible interview. Your hands are sweaty; you look down and discover one black shoe and one brown shoe; you forget the interviewer's name—the list goes on. Now open your eyes and relax. You already know how to avoid these obvious interview pitfalls by preparing thoroughly. You've released nervous energy

before arriving; you've taken the time before your interview to dress professionally; and you repeated the interviewer's name out loud or silently to yourself during the handshake.

Of course, you are not in the clear yet. Mistakes can be made at any time, and it is important to do all you can to minimize them. Your work does not stop after preparation

Fidgeting in Your Chair

- When you sit down, take the time to make sure you are comfortable and in line with the interviewer.

- Fidgeting is an outlet for nervous energy and is often a distraction for those you are talking with.

- If you need to release nervous energy, do so below the knees where the interviewer cannot see.

- When you cut out fidgeting, you appear calm, confident, and in control of yourself.

Playing with Props

- Like fidgeting, playing with props is an outlet for nervous energy.

- When speaking, playing with props such as pens, cups, or a piece of jewelry distracts from your message.

- You can use a meaningful prop when gesturing, but set it down when you are done making your point.

- If you need to have a prop in your hands, make sure it is a notebook or pen and is held steadily.

for the interview, during the introductions, or even after you are seated at the interview. You have to be aware at all times to make sure body language blunders do not occur absentmindedly.

Let's take some time to review some of the most common body language faux pas to avoid during interviews and what you can do if you notice yourself committing these errors. These bad habits may seem simple and obvious, but nonetheless they pop up in almost all interviews, usually to the surprise of the one committing them.

MAKE IT EASY

Practicing your communication skills in front of a mirror, on videotape, or through mock interviews with friends or a career advisor is a great way to gain awareness of your own problematic tendencies. Seeing your body language with your own eyes is more impactful than being told what you are doing wrong, and you will be more motivated to change.

Face Touches

- Self-touch gestures are made when one part of your body touches another part, usually to calm yourself; excessive hand-to-face contact is a prime example.

- Do not touch your face unless you are thinking or making some other meaningful gesture.

- Many people consider unnecessary face touching bad hygiene and very distracting.

- Make sure you never let your head rest on your hands because this is an obvious sign of fatigue or boredom.

Nervous Habits

- Nervous habits develop out of a lack of awareness and are usually associated with insecure, anxious, or absentminded people.

- Self-touches, such as playing with hair, biting nails, or cracking knuckles, detract from your professional, polished, appearance.

- If you tend to fidget when nervous, try exercising the morning of your important interview to release some of that energy.

- Practice relaxed breathing if you find yourself nervous during interviews.

EVALUATING YOUR INTERVIEWER

Read your interviewer's signals to determine when and how to change the pace

So far you have learned what to do with your own body language to create an open environment and appear confident and professional. This section focuses on what to do when the interviewer displays the signs of boredom, annoyance, or disgust that you are trying to avoid. Are there body language tricks you can do to win the interviewer's favor?

The answer is "Yes," but you must act quickly. You should keep tabs on the interviewer's body language that will allow you to recognize changes in behavior that serve as red flags to indicate you are losing his or her interest. Chances are the interviewer is not as knowledgeable as you have become about the signals a person's body language sends, so you are

Crossed Arms = Uncomfortable

- This closed-off body language *might* indicate that the interviewer is not agreeing with what you are saying or does not feel a connection to you.

- Check your body language to make sure that you are maintaining an open position.

- This would not be a time to use mirroring to establish rapport.

- Try engaging the interviewer in active conversation that forces him to gesture instead of allowing his arms to stay crossed.

Tapping Fingers or Toes = Annoyed

- This fidgety body language is a *possible* sign of impatience or annoyance.

- If you are talking too much, begin to make your final point or ask an open-ended question to the interviewer.

- Don't let this aggressive move intimidate you into

adopting closed-off body language.

- Keep your arms and legs uncrossed and be sure you are not dominating the conversation but rather are encouraging two-way communication.

at a slight advantage. What will you do with your new power of educated observation?

When evaluating your interviewer's body language, look for clusters; it is not enough to conclude that the job is out of your reach because the interviewer is not giving you proper eye contact. You should look for at least two, preferably three "red flags" before settling on any inference based on the interviewer's body language.

YELLOW LIGHT

Remember that no body language move is conclusive in and of itself. Many men feel comfortable leaning back in a chair; many women are taught to sit with crossed legs, and let's face it: Everybody has to yawn at some point. Just because your interviewer displays one of these "taboo" moves does not indicate a lost cause. It may be your cue to change the pace or ask a question based on your observations.

Leaning Forward, Engaged

- The comfortable body language of the interviewer probably means that the interview is going well.

- You can mimic the interviewer's body language by leaning forward to reciprocate his or her interest.

- Because you have the interviewer on your side, you can ask one of the tougher questions you prepared, such as concerning salary or benefits.

- If the interviewer leans back at the mention of one of these subjects, take a step back to your previous behavior.

Slouching, Wandering Eyes

- This passive posture and lack of eye contact are a red flag; you need to change something quickly to win back the attention of the interviewer.

- Remember that the interviewer's apparent lack of interest could be due to boredom, tiredness, preoc-cupation, or some other factor.

- It is best to make him or her move to feel more involved and awake.

- Try asking an open-ended question, creating a visual by gesturing, or otherwise engaging the interviewer.

FOR THE INTERVIEWER

The interviewee is not the only one who should consider conscious and subconscious body language signals

Let's take off the *interviewee* hat and try on the hat of the *interviewer*, which hasn't received much attention thus far. You may think, "The interviewer isn't the one trying to land the job, so why would his body language even matter?"

Whether you are looking for a candidate with confidence, extensive knowledge, or heartwarming friendliness, you definitely want the interviewee to be sincere in what he portrays. Picking a candidate with an appealing facade who turns out to be a nightmare wastes time, money, and resources.

As the interviewer, you have the power to set the initial mood of the interview. Your best bet is to make the interviewee feel comfortable in the beginning to be himself so

Avoid Talking Excessively

- The point of interviewing is to get to know the interviewee and see how he interacts in a professional setting.

- You should talk 20 percent of the time; the other 80 percent of the time the interviewee should be talking or you should be asking open-ended questions.

- Maintain open body language with lots of palm-up gestures so the interviewee feels comfortable sharing thoughts and questions.

- When listening, tilt your head and nod periodically.

Don't Be an Open Book

- Present a neutral demeanor in the first minutes of the interview.

- Your body language should allow your interviewee to feel comfortable and open so you can get a feel for his or her natural personality.

- Appear friendly but avoid the "perma-smile"; instead, let your interviewee earn your full smile by saying the right things.

- Stay neutral but friendly until something sparks your interest. Then lean forward to show your interest.

you can get an accurate read on if or where he would fit in at your company. After you have an idea of what the person is like, you can alter the atmosphere to see how he reacts in different scenarios. If you are looking for someone who is comfortable with the frontline of sales, you may want to increase pressure during the interview to see how he handles it. The possibilities with body language are endless; just apply what you've learned to get the atmosphere you want.

· · · · · · · · · · · · GREEN ● LIGHT · · · · · · · · · · · ·

Some interviewers like to see how the interviewee's body language holds up when given a push to fall into bad habits. For example, you can set a clicky pen on the interviewee's side of the desk, give the interviewee a chair with no arm rests, or lean back and tap your fingers on the desk. The job position may entail all of these scenarios, and it is useful to know how each candidate will react.

Regulate Pressure

- As the interviewer, you are in control of the level of pressure throughout the interview.

- To decrease pressure, avoid silence when writing notes. Say something like, "Okay, so you have lots of frontline sales experience" as you write.

- To increase pressure, stay silent while writing notes; the interviewee will feel the need to say something if uncomfortable with silence.

- To minimize pressure, space questions throughout the interview; machine-gun questioning at any one time will create stress.

Avoid Group Interviews

- Group interviews sound appealing when trying to save time but do not create an open and fair atmosphere for everyone.

- Group interviews often result in one or two aggressive people dominating the attention of the interviewer.

- A one-on-one interview allows you to direct your attention fully to one person at a time.

- If you must conduct a group interview, give everyone equal attention by directing questions to individuals and turning your body to face each speaker.

AMERICAN GESTURES: TRANSLATED

When abroad be aware that your gestures are likely to have different meanings

When traveling abroad, you must be aware that the meanings of gestures vary from country to country. Make a conscious effort to watch how you move and don't make any hand signals that you aren't sure about. Some movements and even well-intended gestures may be considered offensive. Be cautious with one of the most classic American hand

symbols, the thumbs up, because in some places it is a terrible offense. As another example, do not show the soles of your feet in an Arab country, Turkey, Korea, or Thailand. It is considered to be rude.

The images below show four gestures that are widely used in the United States. Do not assume that these are universal.

Stop/Halt

- The hand held up with palm facing out is a universal sign for stop.

- In Greece, however, it is an insult that means "go to hell."

- In the Caribbean and parts of Africa, this emblem translates into "you have five fathers"—the equivalent of calling someone a bastard.

- Whether you intend for it to signal "stop" or the number five, be careful where you use this symbol abroad.

A-okay

- This emblem means "everything is okay" in the United States.

- In Germany it has dual meanings. Although it is recognized as "okay," it can also be used offensively.

- In Japan it means "zero" or "money." In Venezuela, Peru, Russia, and the Mediterranean, it is a sexual insult.

- In Arab countries it is the "evil eye." In France and Belgium it signifies worthlessness.

As a tourist, you may want to either make a conscious effort to limit your hand movements in order to avoid misinterpretation or to learn what common gestures are used in that country. Politicians and diplomats meeting abroad should also watch their hand signals. They tend to use encouraging hand gestures or emblems such as the "thumbs up," "v for victory," or "a-okay" signs to generate positivity among public crowds. Doing so can be disastrous if an illustrious political figure makes one of these gestures in a foreign country where it signifies something vulgar or offensive.

CULTURAL CUES

Thumbs Up

- In the United States, the "thumbs up" sign is used frequently and signifies approval.

- It has the same meaning in many countries, including Canada, Ukraine, and Russia.

- It specifically means "okay" in France, Paraguay, and Uruguay.

- It is highly offensive in Israel, Kuwait, and Saudi Arabia. Try smiling to show approval instead in these countries.

V for Victory

- In the United States, this sign means "victory" or "peace." It was first used during World War II and has been presented facing both inward and outward.

- In some places it is the equivalent of the American middle finger "flicking off."

- It is considered obscene when flicked with palm inward in United Kingdom and is known as "the two-fingered salute."

- It is also offensive in New Zealand, Australia, South Africa, and Ireland.

FORMAL GREETINGS

From handshaking to embracing to bowing, socially acceptable forms of greeting vary among cultures

Formal greetings are important to establish recognition, trust, and respect between people who are either newly meeting or revisiting each other. Most Westerners use the handshake to greet, and this is quickly becoming a trend all around the world in business settings. But don't be alarmed when you travel out of the country, and a stranger looks at your outstretched hand with a blank expression. Instead of holding out a hand, he may step back and take a bow or even kiss your cheeks depending on his nationality.

Just as the handshake can be given in many different styles that communicate certain attitudes or statuses, other gestural formal greetings can be similarly varied.

Handshake Differences

- As shaking hands has become world-wide in business, you must be aware of handshake differences between cultures.

- A left handshake would be a serious offense in Arab culture. Offering the left hand for nearly anything is offensive in this region.

- In Denmark women's hands are to be shaken prior to men's, and children there are taught to use the handshake at an early age.

- The British prefer a brief, firm shake. The French prefer a light, single shake that is quickly withdrawn. And the Germans like a firm, quick pump of the hand.

Bowing

- The bow is practiced in Japan, Korea, and several other countries of the East.

- In Japan it is called the "kowtow" and is an essential practice in society.

- The depth of the bow varies in degree to show respect; a superior may just nod.

- The bow is also used in degrees of frequency and duration to express apology or thanks. When handshaking in Asia, a small bow may be included.

Pay attention to proxemics (space) and haptics (touch) during formal greetings in different cultures. People avoid touching and have larger zones of personal space in many cultures, such as Japan, where people bow. Other cultures, such as in Italy or France, may be more comfortable with touching and have smaller spatial boundaries and so the kissing of the cheeks is not out of the ordinary.

People in most Asian countries either use a form of bowing or put their hands in a steeple form (as if praying) or a combination of the two in greetings.

Most of the world does not traditionally greet by handshakes. In Greece backslapping often takes the place of handshaking. In some parts of Tibet sticking the tongue out is a friendly greeting. Native Hawaiians greet affectionately with the "aha" by hugging and exchanging breaths. In Zambia some greet with a thumb squeeze.

The Wai

- The Wai is a Thai greeting in which hands are placed in a prayer position at the chin and accompanied by a slight bow.

- In Cambodia and Laos, the hands in prayer are placed at the chest and followed by a bow.

- The greeting derives from spiritual practices and is a symbol of respect.

The Anjali Mudra

- The Anjali Mudra is an Indian formal greeting.

- It is formed with hands at the chest in prayer formation with a slight bow of the torso accompanied by slight bow of the head.

- The greeting is often accompanied by the word "namaste."

- The greeting is also used to open and close yoga exercise in many cases.

CULTURES CLOSE UP

Take a look at the Arabs and Italians first to see how those cultures differ in body language

Let's travel to four countries and observe body language.

You are in Saudi Arabia, where dignity and respect are pillars of society. Islam dominates this Arab culture, influencing social behavior to be based in generosity, respect, and solidarity. Nonverbal communication plays a major role because Saudis rely on cues such as eye contact, silence, and tone of voice. Eye contact and close proximity are the norm, though discretion must be observed when communicating with a Saudi woman. Silence is a sign of wisdom and even superiority. Silence may be accompanied by an Arab holding his chin with the thumb of the right fist to indicate contemplation. The gesture conveys insight and maturity. You may see men

Male Handhold

- It is not uncommon for men to hold hands in Arab counties as a friendly gesture.

- Hand-holding is normal because of the closer boundaries between Arab men, and it is a gesture of solidarity.

- It can be offensive to lean away from an Arab, and if an Arab won't touch you, he probably thinks you are untrustworthy.

- Given the American homosexual connotation of this gesture, the young men of these cultures are lessening that tradition.

Arab Respect

- We say, "I cross my heart" or use "Hand on my heart" as an expression.

- In Arab countries people actually place their hand on their heart to show genuine respect and humility.

- They accompany the gesture with the words "al-Hamdu li-Ilah" ("praise be to God").

- Sometimes this is used in combination with a small bow, meaning "thank you."

holding hands as a habit of friendship. Do not use your left hand in any circumstance because it is considered unclean and offensive. Do not use the "a-okay" sign because it is an insult or curse that refers to the "evil eye."

You are in Italy going to a dinner party. The host greets you with an embrace and will touch each of his cheeks alternately to yours and maybe kiss them slightly. Be prepared to be touched often and to have your personal space crowded. At dinner (which may last hours) the Italians will gesture almost constantly with their hands while conversing. They use hundreds of emblematic hand gestures, and you should study them if you desire to communicate in Italian. Don't be alarmed if you are interrupted and an Italian pins your hand to the table or presses your arm to take the speaking cue. An Italian may speak very close to your face. If you are excessively quiet or still, Italians may wonder if something is wrong with you or if you are ill. They may interpret this behavior as cold and unfriendly.

Italians

- Italians use highly demonstrative, expressive, and pronounced body language, the most use of all European nations.

- They can be perceived as exaggerated or even aggressive by non-Italians.

- Touch is more common, and they have smaller proximities.

- Hand gestures are abundant and used almost constantly, often in place of words.

Italian Questioning

- One popular Italian gesture is the palm facing in with the tips of the fingers gathered as if holding a marble with the wrist shaking up and down.

- It means, "What do you want?" or "What the heck are you saying?"

- This gesture is also common in Italian-American communities.

- When incredulous at the stupidity of what someone is saying, nothing expresses irritation or disbelief better than this recognizable gesture.

CULTURES CLOSE UP (CONT.)

Now let's look at the English and Japanese to explore more differences in communication

Now you are in England. England is dominated by class differences, and you will see a wide range of nonverbal behavior, though expression is primarily verbal. You catch a glimpse of a newspaper headline that reads, "British Airways Staff Told to Relax and Lose Those Stiff Upper Lips." The stereotype of the dry, reserved English with the "stiff upper lip" is that they use less body language, harnessing and limiting their physical movements or at least not drawing attention to them. At the worst they may appear cold to foreigners. You read the article, and it says the airline's staff is to be trained by body language experts to improve customer relations. Unlike the Italians, the English do not excessively wave their hands around and are

English Stiff Upper Lip

- The stiff upper lip appears when the lips are pursed and appear smaller, and the cheek muscles are tensed.

- This is an iconic British expression, and it allows them to mask their emotions.

- It causes many in outside cultures to view British as overly cold.

- They are known to be reserved, and touching, especially strangers, is not at all okay. Boundaries are farther, and expression is primarily verbal.

The English View

- Traditionally and stereotypically, the English view hand gestures in communication with deep suspicion.

- They may view them as signs of theatricality (insincerity), effeminacy, or foreign extraction.

- English tend to keep their hands firmly to their sides in conversation. But the hands should be in sight at all times because it is considered impolite to talk to anyone with the hands in the pockets.

- They use hand gestures only when absolutely necessary, though this practice is changing.

often seen holding them behind their backs, which can be perceived as restraint or formality. Personal space is wider, and facial expressions such as laughing may appear to be more controlled to an outsider. The Brits do not like to display their feelings. They display friendliness but are not over-the-top enthusiastic. Their body language is moderated.

Your last trip is to Japan. You may perceive the controlled or minimized body movements of the Japanese such as the low-postured stride in the image below, the bow, or shifting eye contact as timid and passive behavior. However, these characteristic Japanese behaviors reflect humility and respect. If your movements are too overt and expansive, the Japanese may find you arrogant, ungraceful, or obnoxious.

Although Japanese businesspeople will accommodate Western style, they maintain ceremonious practices such as hierarchical seating arrangements, a preference for traditional bowing over handshaking, a formal rigid posture, and a ceremonial delivery of business cards. Receive a business card with much grace and care. Don't crumple it or immediately shove it into your pocket.

Japanese Walk

- The Japanese traditionally walk with short, quick strides and drooping shoulders.

- This low posture is called "*teishisei.*"

- For an American going to Japan, this would appear to be a sign of weakness and low confidence, but in fact it is a sign of humility and respect.

- In contrast, Americans view walking tall with longer strides and a more upright posture as displaying confidence and strength.

Japanese Talk

- When Japanese converse, their eyes tend to shift away, resulting in inconstant eye contact.

- This is perfectly normal in Japan. In America establishing eye contact during a conversation shows interest, honesty, and sincerity.

- Avoidance of eye contact in the United States would show that you weren't interested, were dishonest, or were trying to be sly.

- In Japan the opposite is true; eye contact shows that you are being aggressive, rude, or insistent to be equal or belligerent.

MANNERS & ETIQUETTE

Be a professional tourist; mind your manners all around the world and be welcomed

Social rules and conventions such as etiquette influence the way we move our bodies around and determine what is acceptable and what is not, what is obscene, disgusting, or disrespectful, and what is pleasant and appropriate. These rules vary vastly from culture to culture.

In China and Japan, for example, spitting on the street is not uncommon. But don't blow your nose into a handkerchief in Japan; handkerchiefs are only for wiping skin. If you must, use a tissue but try not to "blow" too loudly because doing so may seriously disturb passersby.

Touching the head of people from predominantly Buddhist countries is also a no-no. Some cultures have preferences

Dirty Shoes

- Exposing the sole of the shoe or sole of the foot can be considered rude or filthy.

- It is frowned upon in France, Thailand, Japan, and the Middle East.

- As the lowest part of the body, the foot is seen as insulting when brought to view.

- Many Americans sit with a foot exposed and are cautioned to rein in their feet and keep them firmly on the ground or facing the ground when traveling abroad.

No Head Patting, Please

- Patting a Buddhist on the head is rude.

- The head is considered the repository of the soul in many countries where spirituality is important.

- Refrain from patting children's heads—it will not be viewed as an affectionate or warm gesture.

- Actually, patting almost anyone on the head in any culture is considered, if not rude, a little odd and somewhat belittling.

over how the hands are used. Arabs do not touch people or food with the left hand, and Japanese use two hands to pass items to others. Showing respect is a form of etiquette that varies from country to country. In many cultures people rise out of their seats and stand to pay respect. In countries that use the bow, it is used not only to greet but also to show respect. The deeper the bow, the more respect. It may also be used to express apology. In the United States people are trained from a young age to look others in the eye and give a firm handshake to establish polite and respectful rapport.

Finger Pointing

- In the United States, pointing at a thing in some cases is acceptable, whereas pointing at people is considered rude.

- Pointing with the index finger is rude in the Middle East and Far East.

- Use the thumb instead with an open hand to point.

- Don't be surprised when people in some cultures, such as some Asians and Italians, use the middle finger to point.

Japanese Item Passing

- Passing an item to someone with one hand is rude in Japan.

- Always use two hands.

- Whether the item is as small as a utensil or a pen or as big as a water jug or a bottle of liquor, still remember to use two hands, even if you are easily able to pass with a single hand.

- Though this custom may seem silly to some, it is just as important, for example, as eating without elbows on the table in Western cultures.

187

NOT-SO-UNIVERSAL FACES
The interpretation of facial expressions has cultural differences; not all faces are universally recognizable

Even though Dr. Paul Ekman classified and identified seven basic facial expressions (anger, disgust, fear, happiness, sadness, surprise, and contempt) that are biologically common among people of all ethnicities, interpretation varies across cultures. What's more, some cultures have trouble expressing some of these emotions on the face.

In cultures where emotional control is the norm, such as Japan, focus is placed on the eyes in order to interpret someone's feelings. In cultures where emotions are openly expressed, such as the United States, the mouth is used to interpret facial expression. Because the eyes convey much subtler messages than the mouth (which is the most

Emoticons

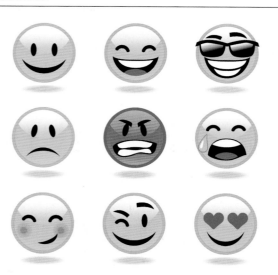

- The U.S. emoticons :) and : (and : o denote happy, sad, surprised faces, respectively.

- Japanese tend to use the symbol (^_^) to indicate a happy face and (;_ ;) or (T_T) to indicate a sad face and (*_*) to indicate surprise.

- Research in a collaborative study between Masaki Yuki (Hokkaido University), William Maddux (INSEAD), and Takahiko Masuda (University of Alberta) found that in cultures where emotion is controlled, such as Japan, focus is placed on the eyes to interpret emotion.

Ambiguous Expressions

- There is one problem with the way the Japanese focus on observing emotion in the eyes.

- Relying solely on the eyes creates ambiguity between fear and surprise.

- It also creates problems in distinguishing anger and disgust.

- Many East Asians have trouble with these distinctions because they are not paying as much attention to the cues that the mouth gives.

188

expressive part of the face), could the Japanese be more effective at detecting lies? Or is this discrepancy a disadvantage because research has shown that they tend to confuse fear for surprise and anger for disgust?

So Ekman is contradicted—are facial expressions genetic, or are they cultural?

Different cultures also have different standards of smiling. Some tend to mask or downplay their facial expressions, and you may find that these people appear elusive or private. Muzzled expressions can be hard to decipher.

Differing Interpretations

- East and Southeast Asian people convey embarrassment by smiling and even laughing. Some Westerners do this when they are nervous.

- A neutral or "impassive" expression may suggest anger in East Asia.

- It is incorrect to interpret this as concealment; these facial gestures are perfectly understood in their own communities.

- By comparison, an impassive expression without eye contact among most, but not all, Native Americans communicates attentiveness and respect.

CULTURAL CUES

Smile Training

- Training sessions in parts of Asia teach people to smile properly by Western standards.

- Some of these sessions tell participants to put a pencil into their mouth to simulate smiling.

- Doing this allows participants to stretch the mouth while also showing their teeth in what is almost universally considered a smile or expression of joy.

- Just because some people don't smile the way you do does not mean they are not happy or joyous.

189

DECEPTIVE DENIALS
Consistency is the key, even if they are consistently lying

Celebrities are constantly in the public eye, their every move being scrutinized, publicized, and analyzed. Consider Angelina Jolie and Brad Pitt's denial of an intimate relationship back in 2003. During a promotional appearance for the film *Mr. and Mrs. Smith*, Angelina displayed the "princess pose"—hands behind back, chin tilted down toward a raised shoulder. She looked at Brad and gazed down and then back at Brad, quickly catching herself and snapping her head to face forward. Although both denied the rumors, Angelina's bashful, flirty, love-struck body language was a far cry from her previous baseline of extreme confidence and independence—a pretty powerful hot spot.

Like other celebrities, politicians are constantly being watched and their behavior analyzed. President Nixon's manner of speech and body language during news conferences regarding Watergate were inconsistent with his usual

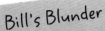

Bill's Blunder

- While denying allegations of an affair, Bill spoke in one direction and pointed in another.

- When he said, "I did not have sexual relations with that woman," he nodded "yes."

- He should have been shaking his head "no," as he did when he said he never told anyone to lie.

- During the trial Bill touched his nose twenty-six times in less than two hours. Although a nose touch does not definitely indicate a lie, this behavior was an extreme deviation from his baseline.

Body Language Inconsistent with Words

- When a person is being truthful and sincere, gestures and words should be congruent in both meaning and timing.

- Meaning consistencies: To convey <u>no</u>, we should shake our head, and we should point in the same direc-tion as we direct verbally; otherwise, we risk sending an inconsistent message.

- Timing consistencies: The gesture should be delivered a fraction of a second before the corresponding word is spoken.

baseline, and the deviations were strong indicators of his guilt to many people. Fast forward two decades to the time following the court ruling that found Bill Clinton guilty of perjury—the Internet was flooded with Clinton's body language tells that Americans should have seen during his public, adamant denials.

Though everyone has 20/20 hindsight, it's difficult to detect a lie at the time it is being told. Analysis of body language is not an exact science but deviations from a well-established baseline are powerful indicators that there is more to the story.

MAKE IT EASY

You are now pretty well versed on body language and its implications when reading people. You know the steps: baseline normal behavior, recognize deviations while considering all possible meanings, then ask direct and open-ended questions to uncover the truth. Take some time to search the Internet for the speeches mentioned in this chapter, taking notes on deviations.

Dick's Deceit

- While speaking during the news conference, Nixon felt comfortably in control, gesturing or placing hands visibly on the podium. This was the baseline he displayed during other less-stressful speeches.

- After "I'm not a crook . . . ," he stepped back, distancing himself from the lie, and crossed his arms defensively.

- He quickly placed his hands behind his back when it was time for questions.

- A camera also caught him rubbing his fingers while clasping; self-touch gestures were unusual for him.

Self-touch Gestures

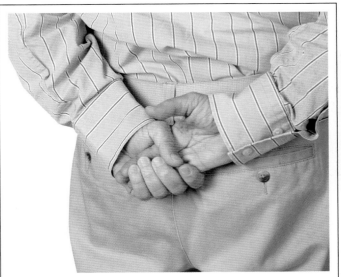

- To review, a self-touch gesture occurs anytime one part of the body touches another —usually to calm nerves.

- Examples: Excessive preening of hair or clothing, wringing of hands, playing with cuticles.

- Those who want to appear calm may put their hands behind their back to hide the self-touch gesture.

- When the hands are relaxed and steady behind the back, this is a sign of confidence; when the hands are fidgety or squeezing tightly, this is a sign of stress.

PUBLICIZED INSINCERITY
Being in the spotlight may change your demeanor, but how much should we expect?

Imagine having to make a lengthy public apology for letting down your family, friends, and those around you. Consider pleading on live television for the safe return of your missing children. What emotions would you be feeling? Would you be able to keep a straight face through the emotions? Would you want to?

Being caught in a lie can destroy the image of a role model. Often when celebrities are facing disgrace and a loss of their fan base, they are told by an advisor that an apology needs to be broadcast in order to win back the public's favor. In the case of Tiger Woods, it seems that he did so simply to appease the public and not because he was intrinsically

Tiger Woods

- Woods was remarkably unemotional while almost directly reading his apology.

- While he claimed to be remorseful, the microexpression of sadness was largely absent.

- The few gestures he used were delivered slightly after the corresponding words were spoken, which suggests they were disingenuous and rehearsed.

- While requesting that his wife and kids be left alone, his behavior changed. He looked directly at his audience with microexpressions of anger and sadness, gestured appropriately, and strayed from his otherwise monotone voice.

Lack of Warranted Emotion

- People should deliver emotional speeches, even loosely scripted ones, speaking mostly from the heart, glancing down briefly at the end of thoughts.

- Sincerity should be apparent through the use of natural gestures and speech directed at the audience and the presence of appropriate microexpressions.

- Tone of voice should also be congruent with the overall tone of the message. When the speaker is sad, the voice may waver; when the speaker is angry, the voice may be projected through clenched teeth.

motivated. Whether he is sorry for his actions is unclear; his deliverance of the apology to the public left most viewers wanting. The reason for his apparent lack of emotion can be debated, but several hot spots scream insincerity.

The 1994 case of Susan Smith's missing children also involved a highly publicized news conference appearance that turned out to be wholly insincere. Smith went on camera with an appeal to the public for any information regarding the whereabouts of her two young sons. Later that day she admitted to murdering them. In an experiment designed to assess the ability to detect deception in the absence of visual clues, Georgetown students were asked to analyze audio clips of "distressed parents," one of whom was later revealed to be Susan Smith. Eight out of the ten subjects were convinced that Smith was being truthful, but two subjects managed to label her as suspicious because of her strange choice of words. When shown the video along with the audio, the ability to detect Smith's deception was much improved.

Susan Smith

- Smith's fearful and desperate tone of voice matched what would be expected of a mother whose children are in danger.

- However, her unusual choice of words made it seem as if she were speaking about someone else's children.

- Statements such as "Not one moment where I don't think about these boys" and "I can't express how much they are wanted back home" sounded detached.

- Besides the obvious absence of a single tear, Smith displayed no microexpressions of sadness in the forehead, eyebrows, or mouth.

Choice of Words

- Detachment: Smith referred to her children very impersonally, as if they were not even hers.

- Tenses: Using past tense such as "I loved her" when referring to someone who is still believed to be alive may indicate the speaker believes or knows that the person is dead.

- "Left" versus "went": Say the crime scene is the kitchen. A guilty suspect often says, "I left the kitchen" instead of "I went into the living room" to distance himself from the scene.

DIRTY MONEY

Do successful business people and politicians usually act appropriately? How about if they are guilty?

Some people are willing to do whatever they can to get money, even at the expense of others. Of course, like most other dishonest people, embezzlers and schemers do not intend on being caught and will maintain deception for years if necessary.

In a news conference on December 19, 2008, Illinois Governor Rod Blagojevich denied wrongdoing when accused of selling President-elect Barack Obama's Senate seat for his own profit. Blagojevich's behavior during this one news conference ranged from his confident baseline to erratic movements and nervous tendencies. The range was apparent when Blagojevich stopped directly addressing the allegations

Rod Blagojevich

- Blagojevich's decisive word choice was undermined by his uncertain body language—a deviation from his confident baseline.

- Deep swallows, inappropriate pausing: His baseline of a quick rate of speech was interrupted many times, notably when he said, "I have done nothing wrong [. . . pause . . . swallow . . . pause . . .], and I'm not going to quit a job that I've been hired to do."

- Nervous movements: He was constantly swaying and moving his hands from one position on the podium to another very rapidly and without purpose.

Striking Extremes

- As seen with Rod Blagojevich, radically different types of behavior can sometimes be seen in a single speech.

- Unless the individual's baseline is erratic behavior, there is probably a mix of baseline and deviations from baseline scattered throughout.

- When trying to identify which behavior is the individual's baseline, find a time when the words are objective ("I am here today to address recent allegations") or quoted from another person ("Rudyard Kipling wrote . . .").

and moved into a quote by Rudyard Kipling. He stopped his nervous swaying and paused appropriately for effect. His speech was fluent and calm—consistent with his baseline but not with the rest of his conference.

Allen Stanford, who is under investigation for an alleged Ponzi scheme, has been famously unusual in the way he has handled the accusations. After he was compared with the admitted Ponzi schemer Bernie Maddof, Stanford's inappropriately extreme threat to the interviewer, ABC's Charlie Gibson, made him seem a little too angry at the wrong person.

Allen Stanford

- When ABC's Charlie Gibson asked how Stanford felt about his money being compared with the dishonest fortune of Bernie Madoff, he used profanity and said to Gibson, "If you say it to my face again, I'll punch you in the mouth."

- The extreme inappropriateness of the threat was an over-the-top show of anger and defensiveness directed at the wrong person—not likely the behavior of a man who is innocent.

- Stanford later claimed to have been so offended at the comparison that he was upset and confused, not really meaning that he would punch sixty-six-year-old Gibson.

Again, no body language move is decisive in and of itself; a lie cannot be concluded until you (1) prove that the move is a deviation from the individual's baseline, (2) observe a cluster of unusual moves (it is best to find at least three deviations), and (3) ask direct and open-ended questions.

Overcompensation

- **Misplaced anger:** Misplaced anger is often a sign of guilt or fear. Innocent people are more likely to direct their anger over false accusations at those who are making the accusations, leaving other innocent people out of it.

- **Violent anger:** Anger in the form of violence or a threat of violence is overcompensation for guilt or fear, not likely to be shown by an innocent person.

- **Character testimonies:** Those who are covering up guilt often give an unsolicited character testimony such as, "Ask anyone; they'll tell you I'm an honest man."

WE SHOULD HAVE SEEN IT

195

BEFORE & AFTER

We can expect to see some emotion; when we do, is it the right one?

In analyzing people's body language we should always take a baseline of their actions and then compare that to the actions that we would like to understand. In viewing the deviations in people's actions between these two actions it is much easier to see what tells they were displaying.

Incongruence is a significant indicator in deception. If we take a look at the entire picture and ask two questions, we will have a very good indicator of deception. First, does the entirety of the statement make sense and not stray in various directions? Second, do all the aspects of their statement—their body language, their voice (tone, pitch, speed, and volume), and their words—correlate to paint a consistent picture?

Marion Jones

- Marion Jones first claimed to be innocent of the allegations of steroid use during the 2000 Summer Olympics. In her denial she claimed to be "more sad than angry," although neither corresponding microexpression could be seen on her face. Her defiant words were instead coupled with almost constant microexpressions of surprise and fear.

- Jones later admitted to steroid use, acknowledging that she had previously lied both to the news media and justice system. After pleading guilty in court nearly three years later, a tearful Jones addressed the media on the courthouse steps, repeatedly choking up and showing the microexpressions of sadness.

Sincere Emotions

- When a person makes a sincere statement, emotion should be apparent in the tone of voice, facial expressions, and choice of words.

- Jones's denial was unemotional and disconnected, with incongruence in all of the above.

- When she finally admitted to steroid use, you could see the sadness, remorse, and relief in her face, and shame in her shoulders and hear sadness in her wavering voice.

A negative answer for either one of these questions does not immediately indicate deception, but it should lead you to question the statement and the person making it to better understand the reason for the negative answer.

People have a physiological predisposition to tell the truth, which in part is why technology can aid in the detection of deception. It is also part of the reason for the lack in congruence in deceptive statements. Interpersonal communication is such a complex interaction that few people can control every aspect of it in order to deliver a lie that cannot be detected. This is one reason why we tend to see the lack of congruence in deceptive people; as our body wants to tell the truth, we have to consciously alter its language in order to tell a believable lie.

As we view before and after statements we will see that certain pieces of the deceptive communication were not consistent, while in the "after" we do not see significant incongruence in the statements or people.

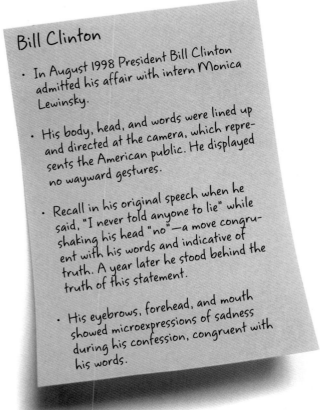

Bill Clinton

- In August 1998 President Bill Clinton admitted his affair with intern Monica Lewinsky.

- His body, head, and words were lined up and directed at the camera, which represents the American public. He displayed no wayward gestures.

- Recall in his original speech when he said, "I never told anyone to lie" while shaking his head "no"—a move congruent with his words and indicative of truth. A year later he stood behind the truth of this statement.

- His eyebrows, forehead, and mouth showed microexpressions of sadness during his confession, congruent with his words.

Back to Baseline

- After the stress of hiding a lie is over, the individual will likely return to baseline behavior.

- Facial expressions, gestures, and tone of voice will match the message.

THE WALK & GREET

This exercise examines strangers' responses to your body language or lack thereof

Let's test our newly learned skills in reading, projecting, and understanding the importance of body language.

In this exercise you will need to plan two separate walks that lead you past at least thirty people. Choose a suitable time and location, such as a shopping mall, route to work, or a popular main street. Each walk should be a minimum of fifteen minutes. Make sure to eliminate as many variables as possible that may taint the exercise, such as inclement weather. Bring a pen and paper to record people's responses.

On your first walk, say, "Hello," "Good morning," or another similar greeting to every person you pass. Give each a hearty smile and a head nod while doing so, making sure you put

The First Walk

- This image exemplifies how you should greet a passerby on your first walk.

- Animate your face with a smile, add a head nod, and say a short, friendly greeting as discussed. Be cheery but don't exaggerate.

- You will observe that most people respond with some form of greeting or at least recognition through body language.

- Note exactly which parts of their body respond, if at all.

What to Expect

- You will observe how people react to you as a cheerful and confidant stranger.

- By observing their body language, you might gain insight into their personality, mood, or destination.

- Extroverts are likely to respond with strong, positive body language, and introverts may not react at all.

- Look for returned verbal greeting, specific eye contact, pausing, head nods, proximal movements, and facial expressions.

your entire body into your gestures. Make sure you record the number of responses you receive and each responder's body language. Is the response audible or just mouthed? Does each responder smile back or present a blank face?

On the second walk, take the same route at the same time of day. But this time refrain from using any body language or voice inflection when greeting people. Again, count the responses you receive for this exercise and make note of each person's body language.

The Second Walk

- This image shows how in the second walk you should simply go by passersby without using any body language.

- Try even eliminating eye contact.

- Maintain a monotonic voice for the greeting by not animating your speech with any emotions or inflections.

- Note the reactions and then compare notes with the first walk.

What to Expect

- You will notice how people react to you as a stiffer, possibly introverted stranger.

- Will they mirror you and be equally as unresponsive with their body language, or will they become animated?

- How many more people reacted to you in the first walk than in the second?

- Do you observe differences in people who seem to rush as opposed to people who calmly stroll?

HANDS-ON EXERCISES

199

THE GROUP EFFECT
The body language of a group as a whole can either include or exclude individuals

The following two scenario exercises highlight the importance of nonverbal gestures in communicating. Furthermore, they illustrate not only that body language is not just a function of individual behavior but also that group body language can be a dictating societal force. Have you ever walked up to a group of people discussing something and

felt like you were included in the conversation, even if you didn't say a word? The group members were probably making eye contact with you, drawing you into the conversation not only verbally but also through proxemics, haptics, and inviting facial expressions.

In this exercise you'll need to coordinate with a friend or

Shut Out

- This image shows the first scenario in the exercise.

- The bystander is being shut out of the communication because of the closed body language of the other two individuals.

- The other two individuals can use shoulder angles to close off the bystander.

- By not being given any eye contact, the bystander is further cut off.

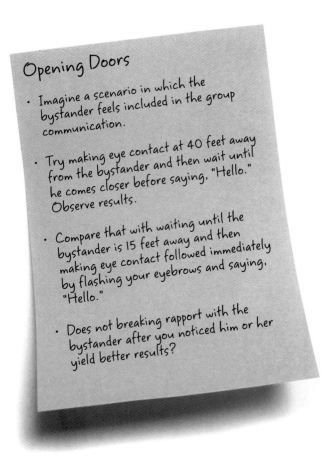

Opening Doors

- Imagine a scenario in which the bystander feels included in the group communication.

- Try making eye contact at 40 feet away from the bystander and then wait until he comes closer before saying, "Hello." Observe results.

- Compare that with waiting until the bystander is 15 feet away and then making eye contact followed immediately by flashing your eyebrows and saying, "Hello."

- Does not breaking rapport with the bystander after you noticed him or her yield better results?

some coworkers to see if you can make people feel included or excluded through the use of body language.

For the first scenario, test the reaction of a friend or colleague by initiating a conversation in which you and another person verbally engage the bystander in communication but block out the bystander by using body language. Face each other and quite literally use your bodies to close the bystander out of the conversation. Observe how the bystander quickly becomes uncomfortable in this situation.

For the second scenario, use body language to keep the group communication completely open by standing in a circular formation and including the bystander in the conversation nonverbally as well as verbally. Notice that the bystander now feels very much a part of the conversation based solely on a change in body language.

Now that you have the knowledge, you can use body language as a tool. This exercise shows how much power your body moves have in determining the outcome of any situation.

Listening without Your Ears

- Now that you've read this book, you should recognize and understand many body language cues. Try watching a taped TV show with no volume.

- Pay careful attention to the body language and take notes to see if you can figure out what happened

based solely on nonverbal communication.

- Watch the taped show again with volume to see if you were correct. If you don't get it correct the first time, remember to take all the actors' entire bodies into account.

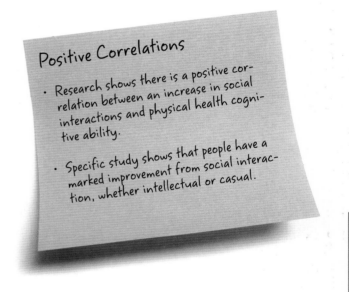

Positive Correlations

- Research shows there is a positive correlation between an increase in social interactions and physical health cognitive ability.

- Specific study shows that people have a marked improvement from social interaction, whether intellectual or casual.

DATING TESTS

Learn empathy through mirroring and learn who makes the first flirtation moves

In order to get a date, go on a date, and engage a date, you should value the importance of two body language functions—mirroring and flirting. Why mirroring? Because when you mirror someone's moves and expressions, you connect to that person and show that you are empathetic or understanding of his or her feelings, thus appealing to his or her emotional sensibilities. And why flirting? Because flirtation not only is an indication of attraction and a dating cue but also enlivens a romance. Let's explore two exercises—one for mirroring and one for flirting.

Get a partner whom you are going to mirror. Also get a third party to observe the mirroring and to let you know if

The First Move

- Conventional standards tell us that a man often make the first apparent move or make the first greeting when interested in a woman.

- After reading this book, you may have picked up on the fact that women have much higher aptitude for body language and tend to be tactical with their moves.

- Given that fact, it is not surprising that women are usually the actual initiators of flirtation.

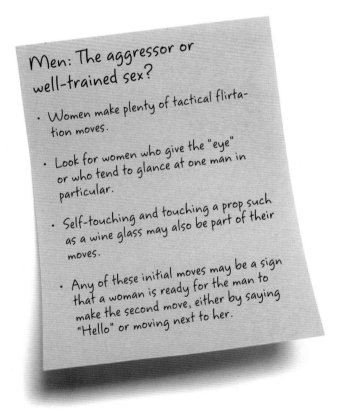

Men: The aggressor or well-trained sex?

- Women make plenty of tactical flirtation moves.

- Look for women who give the "eye" or who tend to glance at one man in particular.

- Self-touching and touching a prop such as a wine glass may also be part of their moves.

- Any of these initial moves may be a sign that a woman is ready for the man to make the second move, either by saying "Hello" or moving next to her.

you've missed anything. Tell the person whom you are going to mirror to think of something that brings strong emotions to mind, to not tell you verbally, and to let those emotions come out through body language—using posture, position, gestures, movements, and expression. Copy every element of body language that this person displays and hold the position. Mirror for three minutes and then pay attention to how you feel. Discuss the emotions with the person you mirrored, and you may be surprised to find that they match.

In our society many people are familiar with the belief that males tend to "make the first move." In this bar room exercise, you may realize differently. Although men do often tend to approach their female counterparts, a closer observation indicates that women actually use subtle body language to lure men and in doing so make the first move. Test this theory by going to a bar, dance, or ballgame—any social place where men and women meet and interact. Watch males and females closely, giving particular attention to who initiates nonverbal communication. See if your preconceived notion of who made the "first move" has changed.

Assessing People

- Assess the person in this photo. What type of person do you think he/she is? If you said auditory you are correct.

- If you see or hear specific indicators of the type of person you are interacting

with, mirror those actions and, if you were correct, a quicker connection will be made.

- People like people like themselves; remembering this will help make that connection quicker.

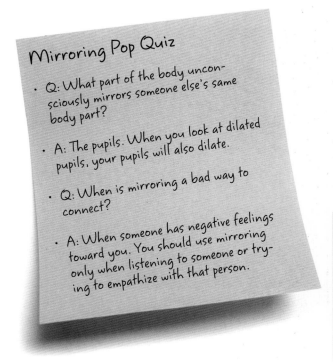

Mirroring Pop Quiz

- Q: What part of the body unconsciously mirrors someone else's same body part?

- A: The pupils. When you look at dilated pupils, your pupils will also dilate.

- Q: When is mirroring a bad way to connect?

- A: When someone has negative feelings toward you. You should use mirroring only when listening to someone or trying to empathize with that person.

STARING CONTESTS

Test your gaze and find out how well you engage in eye contact

Ever wonder where the line between staring and listening intently is? The average amount of time people spend looking at each other during a conversation ranges from 60 to 80 percent. However, people who are speaking tend to look at a listener for less than 50 percent of the conversation, whereas the listener spends over 75 percent on average looking at the speaker. When people increase their average eye contact time, they also increase their level of connection.

Exercise 1. To know what your average gaze time is while speaking and while listening, have somebody use a stopwatch to track the time when you gaze at a speaker. Have the person also track the time when you gaze while speaking. Compare with the times of others. Whoever has the longest gaze time as a listener may be perceived as empathetic and understanding. Those with higher times for gazing while speaking may be perceived as particularly good orators.

The Best Look

- In exercise 1, both speaker and listener should look comfortable, upbeat, and relaxed.

- Look a person in the eyes and maintain as much eye contact as possible without making the person uncomfortable.

- Or rather than trying to maximize your gaze time, find out what your baseline is.

- Relax, don't think about your gaze, and let a third party calculate your natural gaze time while you speak and listen.

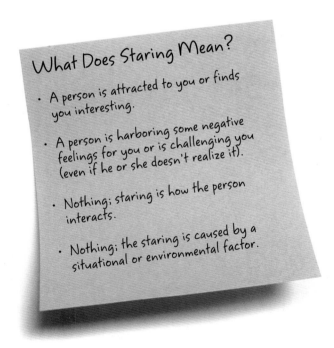

What Does Staring Mean?

- A person is attracted to you or finds you interesting.

- A person is harboring some negative feelings for you or is challenging you (even if he or she doesn't realize it).

- Nothing; staring is how the person interacts.

- Nothing; the staring is caused by a situational or environmental factor.

Exercise 2. As a long-term experiment, engage a person in a conversation regularly. Every time you talk, look the person directly in the eyes and maintain as much contact as possible without making the person feel uncomfortable. Notice how this builds up a stronger relationship, both within that conversation and over time.

Exercise 3. One classic eye game is the staring contest. Here you will test the limits of holding eye contact. Stare someone down until the person retreats. This exercise indicates the power of a gaze as well as the dangers of too much body language.

Exercise 4. The average time of a single gaze is around three seconds, whereas the average mutual gaze is one to two seconds. Figure out how long it takes before your gaze produces anxiety in your partner. To do so, you must first figure out your gaze norm and your conversation partner's gaze norm. The exercise shows that tolerance for staring is very low; anything too far outside of the norm makes for an uncomfortable situation.

Does Anyone Enjoy a Glare?

- In exercise 3, learn to recognize the signs of someone retreating.

- When your stare starts to cause the person anxiety, he or she will show it, as in this image.

- Looking down uncomfortably is a sign of imminent retreat.

- Averting the eyes and engaging in some nervous tick such as a scratch are also a sign.

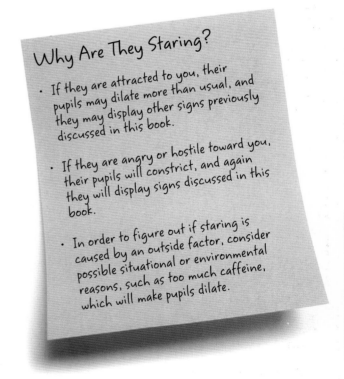

Why Are They Staring?

- If they are attracted to you, their pupils may dilate more than usual, and they may display other signs previously discussed in this book.

- If they are angry or hostile toward you, their pupils will constrict, and again they will display signs discussed in this book.

- In order to figure out if staring is caused by an outside factor, consider possible situational or environmental reasons, such as too much caffeine, which will make pupils dilate.

MIRRORING TESTS
Let's reflect on how we project our thoughts

Do you believe that your body language is simply a result of the feelings behind the words coming from your mouth? Or can it work both ways—your body language is not limited to a reactionary role but can in fact have an effect on your speech? This exercise will give you a better understanding.

First you will select a subject that you are passionate about and find an article about that subject to read aloud. Set up a voice recorder or video camera next to you. Then you will read the article twice, first while standing in front of a mirror keeping your arms comfortably at your side and making an effort not to show any emotion or expression. The second time you will repeat the article using as much body language as possible, including using your arms and expressions on your face.

When you are finished with both read-throughs, rewind the tape and play it back. Notice the difference?

Do You Hear Me?

- To understand someone, even yourself, you may find that there is more to understanding them than just body language; verbiage is also a key piece.

- Phrasing is an important part of the message.

- Now assess someone on your next encounter, and see how much quicker you can build rapport through your phrasing.

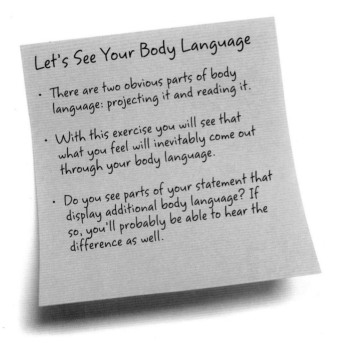

Let's See Your Body Language

- There are two obvious parts of body language: projecting it and reading it.

- With this exercise you will see that what you feel will inevitably come out through your body language.

- Do you see parts of your statement that display additional body language? If so, you'll probably be able to hear the difference as well.

The activity "Can You Feel What I Feel?" will help you achieve both understanding of and confidence in the process of mirroring, one of the most effective body language tools you can employ while establishing rapport. Whether it be a new professional contact, a new friend, or a friendship that you want to turn into something more, rapport is essential to the success of any relationship. It is not enough to simply understand the concept and power of mirroring. You also must practice your skills before you get out on the scene. The key to effective use of mirroring to establish rapport is to make your partner feel that your personalities are naturally alike, not as if you are deliberately mocking or copying him or her.

Can You Feel What I Feel?

- For this activity two participants should be seated next to each other; the chairs should have no arms and be angled slightly toward each other.

- An onlooker should observe from enough distance that he or she is unobtrusive.

- Have the two participants speak about a common interest for two minutes while mirroring one another.

- After two minutes have the two participants as well as the onlooker discuss the atmosphere created by mirroring.

Explanation

- Purpose: To demonstrate the effectiveness of mirroring while building rapport.

- Expected results: The atmosphere should be described as comfortable, familiar, positive, enjoyable, and so forth.

- Have one participant swap out with the onlooker. Move the chairs to be slightly off-set and begin discussion while participants display radically different body language—one gestures, one doesn't; one displays positive facial expressions, one displays negative or no facial expressions, and so on.

- After two minutes discuss the atmosphere. Was it uncomfortable? Negative? Nerve-wracking?

DETECTING DECEPTION
Are you a truth wizard?

These team-building activities exercise many of the skills necessary for effective nonverbal communication.

The following activities are for two or more people and will test and sharpen participants' lie detector skills as well as establish body language ideals that are conducive to a positive atmosphere.

"Two Truths and a Lie" creates a situation in which participants will practice baselining, noticing deviations from a baseline and asking direct and open-ended questions—the three most important skills in reading body language. A "truth wizard" is an individual who can correctly distinguish truths from lies at least 80 percent of the time, whereas the average person is no better than a coin toss. Now that you are well versed on body language, your accuracy should be somewhere between 50 percent and 80 percent.

"Silent Scenario Skits" emphasizes the power of nonverbal

Two Truths and a Lie

- For this activity two participants should be seated directly across from each other; the chairs should have no arms, and there should be no barriers obstructing the participants' view of one another.

- Have participants talk casually for two minutes to gather each other's baseline. After two minutes have each participant prepare three statements—two truths and one lie.

- Participants take turns verbalizing the statements, after which each may have one minute to use questions to uncover the truth.

Two Truths and a Lie Explained

- Purpose: To determine the participants' ability to detect deception.

- Things to consider: Participants should be looking for multiple deviations from his or her partner's baseline that can then be addressed by open-ended questions.

- After lies are revealed, have the participants discuss the baselines they gathered as well as the deviations they observed and repeat the activity if desired.

communication on morale and atmosphere. After one group example, participants are divided into groups to plan additional positive and negative versions of scenarios to act out silently in front of the group. Whether the teams are given preplanned scenarios or asked to think of their own is up to you. Participants should not be discouraged from exaggerating the body language—after all, verbal communication is not an option, and this activity is meant to be fun and creative.

Silent Scenario Skits

- In front of the group, have one participant walk up to another and hand off documents with a large, genuine smile.

- The recipient should give some form of nonverbal thanks (nod head, smile back, and so forth).

- Repeat the handoff but have the participant stomp up to the other and hand off documents with a look of contempt.

- The recipient should be waiting with attitude (weight on one leg, one arm on hip, roll of the eyes, and so forth).

Silent Scenario Skits Explained

- Purpose: To act out positive versus negative body language in real-life, everyday situations.

- Expected results: Participants get a chance to have some fun with body language while seeing how harmful negative body language during coworker interaction can be.

- Divide the group into partners or groups of three to four and allow fifteen minutes for each team to come up with three to five scenarios (depending on the number of groups)—a positive and a negative example for each.

COURTING SUCCESS
Body language and relationships

A professor at Rutgers University and an advisor for the popular dating website Chemistry.com, biological anthropologist Dr. Helen Fisher is a leading specialist in the biology of love and attraction. Her latest book, Why Him? Why Her?: How to Find and Keep Lasting Love, *provides a new way to understand relationships by using a scientifically developed questionnaire to determine your personality type and your compatibility with other types of people, as well as tips on how to find, attract, and keep potential partners.*

Humans, like animals, have developed over time an arsenal of unconscious behaviors and gestures to use when courting a member of the opposite sex. Using research done by anthropologist David Givens and biologist Tim Perper on "the five-part pickup" blueprint and observations made in social hot spots by psychologist Monica Moore, Fisher expands on the subconscious behavior and gestures used in heterosexual courting.

The first step in courting is to establish a territory—a home base—someplace where a person can see and be seen. From there, men and women draw attention to themselves, using body language specific to each gender. Women often remain fairly stationary when displaying courting behavior. Fisher writes that they will primp or touch themselves, smoothing or picking lint off their clothes, massaging a knee, or touching their arm or neck. Props are often used, but only as a potential distraction. Women will engage in the "object caress" as they talk, playing with keys or something on the table. Often a woman will run her fingers or a hand through her hair or expose her neck in an effort to show off her best physical attributes. She may also incorporate licking of the lips or pouting to accentuate her words and draw further sexually charged attention. Many women will act playful or coy—giggling, winking, or batting their eyelashes—as a way to attract attention. Traditionally, women assume the "crouch" position when courting—they hang their heads, turn in their toes, and curl their shoulders, displaying their harmlessness and need of protection.

Courting men, in contrast, tend to display more dominant and mobile behavior. According to Fisher, some men will stride, swagger, or make dominant physical gestures toward other men, such as a punch on the shoulder or a slap on the back. Others will sprawl out in a chair or stand with hands on hips and legs apart to display power and to claim as much space as possible. Men will incorporate objects as women do, but often outdoors and in such a way that will demonstrate their strength, speed, or throwing accuracy. Men will traditionally display the complement of the feminine "crouch" position—the "loom" position—when courting. When a man sees an attractive woman, he will unconsciously straighten up, suck in his stomach, and thrust his chest out in an effort to look large, powerful, and dominant.

Conversation is the third phase in the pickup. Fisher states that women often adopt high, mellifluous tones, while men unconsciously keep their voices low and deep. These specific tones usually appeal to the opposite sex. The best conversation topics are often either compliments or questions because both force the other person to respond and keep the conversation going. Active listening plays a big part in the success of this step because it shows the other person that a conversation partner is interested in what he or she is saying. Eye language and smiling are crucial both before and during conversation—prolonged gazes are used to show interest, and eye contact is important in maintaining conversation and projecting continued interest, while smiling denotes happiness and approachability.

Touching or other physical contact comes next. Fisher states that the woman usually touches first, grazing a man's shoulder, arm, or wrist as she asks a casual question. Depending on his response—whether he turns away, does nothing, or returns the action—she may venture another touch. Some women like to play and will incorporate touching into their fun—tickling a man or covering his eyes from behind. With the right circumstances, the man and woman will eventually increase the amount of casual touching they do.

The final step, known as "interactional synchrony," involves the synchronization of body movement. Fisher explains that as two people

begin to "click," they pivot toward one another, align their shoulders, and exhibit similar motions—as he picks up his beer, she picks up hers and as she crosses her legs, he crosses his. At first two people may move only briefly in synchronization, but eventually they begin to move in tandem more often until they are in perfect rhythm with one another. Fisher observes that this is why singles clubs and bars often have pulsing, rhythmic music and a dance floor—they increase the ease of body synchrony and escalate the courting process.

Choosing a potential target when courting involves more than a conscious realization of who looks attractive. Body language clues assist members of the opposite sex in determining who looks the most approachable and the most likely to reciprocate sexual or romantic interest. However, the effect of these body language clues on a person may vary. Just as "beauty is in the eye of the beholder," there is no one proven body movement that is successful in attracting anyone. Rather, people interested in courting must incorporate numerous movements and gestures into their repertoire, similar to a choreographed dance, in order to succeed.

FACE-TO-FACE TO SOCIAL MEDIA
Using body language to detect fraud

Timothy Pearson is the Executive Director of the Institute for Fraud Prevention where he has learned to become adept at detecting fraud. Dr. Pearson has done research, published articles, and developed courses in the field of fraud prevention. Through his fraud prevention work and his duties as a University professor, Dr. Pearson relies heavily on his knowledge of body language to help him identify fraud, and we discussed how he uses this knowledge in his work and personal life.

Being able to accurately interpret body language is a crucial skill in the field of fraud detection because fraudsters are adept at deception. Understanding the nuances of nonverbal cues is a skill that is becoming lost as we rely more and more on electronic means of communication. Learning how to identify the general behavioral traits of those who are being less than truthful can help fraud investigation experts stop fraudsters in their tracks, and it can help us to remember that there is no substitute for meeting someone in person.

Do you tend to see specific types of people committing fraud? Are there any observable traits?

People tend to hold themselves in a tense posture when they are under stress. Someone who might normally have a lot of confidence in themselves would carry themselves differently than someone who is trying to conceal something. When you are under a great deal of stress you can't control your outward physical manifestations.

Some people are more pre-disposed to succumbing to the financial pressure to commit fraud and they may not be able to find a better way to deal with that pressure so they might make up a lie, or they might make up something to explain their behavior away—a version of cognitive dissonance—we don't want to admit that we are bad people. These people often try to distance themselves from their wrong doing and convince themselves that everything is fine.

Then there is the "accidental fraudster" who was in the wrong place at the wrong time and with the right authority and they pulled the trigger and nothing bad happed the first time so they keep doing They keep doing it until they do not know how to stop. Eventual they get so caught up in it that there is no way to unwind themselve from it.

How much does body language play a role in determining a impression of someone?

Body language plays a huge role in determining first impressions. Yo really do only have one chance to make a first impression. It doe make a big difference even if you have had some previous commu nication with them electronically. The way a person presents him o herself can change your impression of them especially if it is inconsi tent with how they presented themselves online.

A person can seem nice on paper, but if they are difficult to inte act with in person, it could send up a red flag. A person's physic mannerisms are crucial when getting to know them, especially whe it comes to how they align with yours. You have to meet someon in person to know if they are someone you can relate to. Fraudste often con people via the Internet because it is easier to give th impression that they're a really good guy when you don't meet ther in person.

What do you think we rely on to form impressions of peopl when we can't use body language?

I think that the younger generations do not rely on body language i the same way that older adults do. They might rely more on informa tion about people from Facebook, asking themselves, "If I'm going t interact with you online are there six or seven other people that inte act with you online and do they think you're cool?" They don't hav enough data without meeting you, and reading your body languag so they have to turn to other options.

How can you tell when a person is trying to cover something up?

Sometimes the person's voice will trail off and become inaudible when I am interviewing them about an incident. If they are not really being truthful they may make an inaudible statement toward the end of their statement. Dr. Pearson said, "I've been in several situations with students who have committed academic dishonesty. I'm fairly certain when a student sits very comfortably and talks to me without a lot of hand gestures they're innocent. They can still be very upset, but there's a noticeable difference in demeanor in those who don't have anything to cover up."

Can you discuss other instances in your life when you've noticed specific things as far as body language?

There are people who you just know are too uncomfortable to deal with face-to-face for an extended period of time. We, as humans, try to avoid negative events or conflicts if we can smooth them out with body language. So, if there's a way I can throw a softball question first I would do that to feel them out. I think that this has changed with our ability to use email and texting. I think technology makes it far easier for people to interact with others electronically allowing them to avoid the difficulty of dealing with difficult people face-to-face.

What are some circumstances where you might find it preferable to employ body language rather than sending an email?

When you're expressing a position of authority or sympathy, being there in person is more appropriate. These feelings come across through your voice and in the way you present yourself. It really depends on the personality type of the individuals. There are students that I wouldn't meet with alone because I wouldn't want to put myself in danger. Sometimes you just have to tell people things from a distance. It's one of the advantages I think we have in a more wired communication environment. We can choose to share information either in person or electronically.

Do you think there is a greater rise in fraud because of people's constant texting and focusing on their electronic gadgets rather than interacting in person?

When people are texting, and checking Facebook constantly they are not in tune with the people around them. They become oblivious to the dynamics of human interaction. I have a theory that because people are depersonalized by technology they might be more predisposed to fraud. If you feel less of a human connection you might feel less guilt. I would imagine that it could lead you to do things more in your own interest, and lead you to do bad things with less thought about the consequences.

Body language plays a significant role in all of our human interactions. In the realm of fraud investigations understanding the nuances of body language can help an investigator detect fraud, but being well versed in nonverbal communication can also help you to really get to know a person beyond what you can see on your phone or computer's screen.

CROSSING A CULTURAL DIVIDE
Body language helps one immigrant rise to the top

Benjamin Wey emigrated from China to Oklahoma to attend high school with nothing more than one suitcase full of clothes and two suitcases bursting at the seams with books of all kinds. Wey came to the land of opportunity with very little support, money, or friends, and managed to successfully work his way through the American educational system, and overcome all barriers in his path to become the head of the New York Global Group, the only Wall Street advisory firm to be headed by a bilingual Chinese American. He is not a household name (yet), but Wey wears so many hats that he is the perfect example of all that a man can be and what can be accomplished through the simple act of learning the meaning of body language.

A businessman who spans the globe

Benjamin Wey is a Wall Street professional, a professor at two Chinese universities, the proud father of three small children, a husband, a friend, and a chameleon who moves seamlessly between the Chinese and the Wall Street business worlds thanks to his broad understanding of body language variances in both cultures and all that they have to teach us. He is worldly, educated, refined, and wise beyond his thirty-nine years. Wey's vast cultural body language knowledge comes from years of trials, tribulations, and successes.

Bridging the gap between worlds with body language

Wey was able to navigate between the two very different worlds of Chinese and Wall Street business and rise to the top of both by observing people and their body language. Because he is a quick study, Wey easily learned the major differences among people, cultures, and businessmen by watching the way people behave and act in work situations.

"Body language teaches us everything about a person," Wey says. "My professional career would be completely different if it were not for body language and my understanding of it." With one foot in American traditions and the other in Chinese traditions, Wey learned to always be a quiet observer and to follow the cultural norms and social movements dictated by various situations, which helped him become a global success story.

"For example, in China, businessmen are very reserved, quiet, and composed, so much so that it is often hard to read them," Wey says. "There are not a lot of facial emotions that come across, like a Westerner would use." This is because the Chinese in general are low-key and restrained with regard to their emotions; when Wey does business in China, he listens more and talks less. Comparatively, when Wey is among the Wall Street tycoons, he freely uses hand gestures, he more open with his facial expressions, and he knows and expects the business environment to be one in which people are more prone to speak up; the American culture tends to talk more and listen less.

Making body language work for you

Wey's mastery of these two cultural forms of expression through body language gives him an advantage when moving between the two worlds.

"I think it [the body language differences in China and the U.S] very good for me," Wey says, "because my personal experiences have made me more focused on what I change when going between the two cultures; it reminds me that all people want to be treated with respect."

Wey makes body language work to his advantage in each and every setting. At business meetings (regardless of country), Wey always chooses to sit in the seat that faces the best view of the room so that he knows the person he meets with—the one sitting opposite him—looks only at him and listens to what he has to say.

Other times, he tweaks his body language to fit the country that he is in. In China, for example, a seasoned businessman knows t leave ample food on his plate and on the table at business meeting because it sends a subtle message that you respect the fact that the meeting is about work, not food, fun, or alcohol. This gesture also shows that you have been around for a while and are experienced in the ways of the local business culture.

"When you go to business parties, you are there to get a job done so don't focus on the coffee, food, or whatever. Do not focus on the steak. Focus on your job."

Body language as the key to Wey's professional success

Body language has been a leading force in the professional evolution of this international businessman. As all cultures and countries use some type of body language to communicate and subtly convey emotions, it has consistently been the key to Wey's success. Without his ability to blend in on Wall Street and blend in at a university or boardroom in China, Wey would not have had the success he's had.

"Nobody looks at me as a foreigner when I go to China, and no one looks at me as a foreigner when I am in America, so I benefit from both cultures no matter where I go," Wey says.

Key takeaways

Wey has not only taken the time over his career to learn about and understand body language, but he has also gone the extra step to learn to make it work to his advantage. Wey is not privy to any big secret that the rest of us do not know; he is just proof that when you take the time to observe and learn from others' body language and your own, the sky is the limit.

"Listen first, and then react. My college mentor told me to be a better listener and that benefited me my entire life."

THE NEW BODY LANGUAGE
How it can transform your life and relationships

Janine Driver is the author of You Say More Than You Think, *which has been translated into eight languages, and is the president of the Body Language Institute. A dynamic speaker and passionate trainer, Janine incorporates her law enforcement experience into her programs to help people benefit from the knowledge of nonverbal communication in all aspects of human interactions. We shared a lively conversation about the power of nonverbal communication to change lives for the better.*

Because our body language plays such a major role in communication, people should take the time to learn about the new body language and how it can help enhance personal and professional relationships and even save lives.

What is new body language?

There is an often misquoted study about body language that says 93 percent of communication is nonverbal, but that is true only under high stress, emotionally charged situations. What Driver is referring to when she is describing nonverbal communication among people is "the new body language," that is the facial expressions, gestures, and the ways in which we move and hold our bodies. About 50 percent of communication between human beings is verbal and the other 50 percent is nonverbal, our word choices greatly influence body language and vice versa.

The new body language combines both words and body language to get what you want out of life. For example, if a child running in the street, a parent might say, "Billy, don't run in the street. Don't run in the street!" But what is the child hearing? "Run in the street. Run in the street!" The verbal message and what the parent really wants the child to do are incongruous. A better directive would be to say, "Billy, stay on the sidewalk," and then make sure that the body language matches the message with a palm down gesture that communicates clearly that this is an emergency and he must stop now.

Reading body language is the foundation of effective communication

Body language is that secondary layer of communication. Body language is the foundation, but the foundation itself is not of much use without the rest of the building. Recognizing a person's baseline, which is their normal behavior while not under stress, 'hot spots' which refers to unconscious, physical movements that could signal deception, and asking powerful questions about what you are seeing is where the magic happens. All of these elements are necessary to be a powerful communicator.

Becoming knowledgeable about the new body language can change the trajectory of your destiny. It's not enough to just know about body language, or take a 'cookie-cutter' approach to assessing a person's demeanor. It is important to know a person's base line, be observant when something changes and then ask powerful questions to discover what they are really thinking.

Learning the new body language from the inside out

As you ask questions of yourself, such as "What is my baseline? Am I confident, insecure, or arrogant? How do I show up in the world? What is my Perceived Value (PV)?" Your perceived value represents how you value yourself. As your PV increases, you will begin to become more aware of the messages that your physical presence is sending to others. Your PV opens doors and closes doors. It gets people to notice you or to just walk on by you. The new body language begins from within.

What can we learn about others from reading their body language?

The new body language helps you to develop rapport with people. When you understand the nuances of the new body language people will tell you in minutes what it might take therapists years to find out. For instance, a woman wonders why she has trouble connecting with people and making friends. Then she discovers that she ha been squinting and scrunching up her nose—which is a nonverbal cue for disgust—when she meets people because her she has poor eyesight. Her crumpled up nose was coming across as dislike to some people.

But what about those people who are unable to pick up on the nuances of nonverbal communication? How can they make use of new body language? Many people diagnosed with Asperger's syndrome fall into this category. Considered by some to be a mild form of autism, Asperger's syndrome is described by the Autism Society as social awkwardness, not understanding conventional social rules, and displaying a lack of empathy. While children with Asperger's have good language skills, they may not "understand the subtleties of language, such as irony and humor, or they may not understand the give-and-take nature of a conversation." Their inability to pick up on nonverbal cues and their lack of ability to produce the socially-acceptable responses to the emotions of others can cause conflicts in their lives.

Kids with Asperger's are not adept at reading nonverbal communication. Janine Driver's book, classes, and DVDs have given parents of children with Asperger's the tools to help their children learn how to read nonverbal cues in others. These kids can memorize and learn basic tools for interpreting nonverbal communication.

Driver plans to create a series of free resources to help parents of children with Asperger's to learn how to relate better to others in social situations. While they may not feel the empathy in their heart, they can learn to interpret the physical cues of others and respond in a socially appropriate way.

How new body language saves lives

James Cavanaugh, a retired ATF agent, used his intimate knowledge of new body language to persuade David Koresh to release the women and children he held hostage in the Branch Davidian standoff in Waco, Texas.

Using those same skills, Cavanaugh convinced a man who had explosives strapped to his chest to surrender. By watching the feed from a robotic camera, Cavanaugh could see that the suspect was pacing back and forth in an agitated manner. The suspect was trapped in a building with no air-conditioning, surrounded by the police. Cavanaugh offered him a bottle of water so that the man could get hydrated and clear his head. The suspect first smelled the bottle, then tasted a bit of it and spit it out to make sure it wasn't tainted. After the suspect discovered that the water was safe and drank it, he surrendered a few moments later.

The suspect's life was saved, and a building was not blown up because of one law enforcement officer's knowledge of and use of the new body language.

What is one of the greatest lessons we can learn from studying body language?

We can learn how we have been getting it wrong by simply trying to look at body language without incorporating base-lining and asking questions for so many years. People have often misinterpreted nonverbal cues because they did not recognize the differences that govern individual behavior. We don't know how much we have lost by not understanding the power of baselining and asking powerful questions, which are the hallmarks of the new body language. Janine Driver's passion is using nonverbal communication but also combining it with powerful language to get to the truth.

JOB INTERVIEWS & THE WORKPLACE
The role of body language in the interviewing process

Don Rabon is an expert interviewer, interrogator, rapport builder, deception detector, and investigative discourse analyst. The author of Interviewing and Interrogation *and* Investigative Discourse Analysis, *and the coauthor of* Persuasive Interviewing, *Rabon is the owner of Successful Interviewing Techniques, a training and coaching company.*

We spoke to Rabon about the role of body language in the interviewing process and how we can use nonverbal cues to detect deception.

Body language is everything that is involved in the communication process without the linguistic aspects of what people say and how they are saying it. It's what would come across if you were looking at a person and his behavior with no sound to accompany the visual image.

It's important to keep in mind that within the context of an interview setting, both the interviewer and the interviewee have an effect on each other based on their nonverbal communication. At the beginning of the interview, how the interviewee reads the interviewer's nonverbal behavior has a great deal to do with the success of how that interview is going to go. People can't always clearly articulate the sense they get from someone's nonverbal communication, but it doesn't make it any less real and it doesn't mean that they are not going to respond accordingly to the impressions that they receive from that person.

We are working on putting into place a split screen video of an interview with a camera on both the interviewer and the interviewee so that the interviewer can have some sense of how he comes across to the individual that may not be in line with how he thinks he comes across. If an interviewer has made up his mind as to the guilt or innocence of the interviewee as he goes into that interview, the interviewer's nonverbal behavior will reflect that impression prior to the actual line of inquiry, and the individual will respond to that. In a trial, the jury will want to see both what the interviewer saw and what the interviewee saw.

Body language can be used as a tool to help us by being able to show people how to come across as open and how to come across as someone who is there simply to determine what happened or to determine the facts as opposed to passing judgments on the individual being interviewed. It's about changing the mind-set of the interviewer as he goes into the interview. It is important to come across as if you have not yet made up your mind. Rather than coaching people about body language, it is important that people approach the interview process with an open mind so that they come across as open during the interview.

Today, there is a thinning of interpersonal communication between people because they spend more time online and in "virtual" environments. People's innate ability to relate to one another verbally and nonverbally will suffer as people spend more and more time online than they do actually interacting with people in person.

When it comes to body language, in some cases a little bit of knowledge is a dangerous thing. People willing to put in the time to study nonverbal communication can do very well, especially when it comes to detecting deception in interviews. With deception, there are subtle complexities in a person's behavior, such as "high-load" lies, which are lies that tend to decrease the kinesics, or stress shifts of nonverbal behavior. Then you have what are known as "low-load" lies, which tend to increase the kinesics of nonverbal behavior. A lie that might be a "low-load" lie for one person might be a "high-load" lie for another person.

Depending on the environment, society puts an implicit emphasis on nonverbal communication, but on a conscious level society doesn't place a lot of emphasis on it. We are unconsciously interpreting nonverbal behavior constantly in our everyday interactions with other people. We live in such a multimedia world, which leads to more multitasking during human interactions. People who are multitasking may think they are doing things well, but in actuality they are really just not paying attention to others.

Sometimes interviews take a long period of time; you must pay attention and attend to the other person's vocal, verbal, and nonverbal behavior to think about what the individual is saying as opposed to what you know.

The value of being able to interpret nonverbal behavior cuts across all areas of our personal and work relationships, not just in interviews. It is important to be conscious of how you come across to the people who work with and for you, and to be able to pick up on the clues in the nonverbal behavior of the people in your workplace. In marriage, knowledge about nonverbal behavior helps a couple to be able to read one another's cues, but there can be just as much miscommunication nonverbally as there is vocally.

Everyone is somewhat of a body language expert, but we have to take the nonverbal communication within the context that it occurs. Take into consideration other context clues aside from just the nonverbal communication that the person displays in order to find out what is really going on. Use questions to clarify your perceptions so that the person can articulate what he actually thinks.

A piece of advice to share with people who are just starting out in their careers: If you want to be happy and successful, find a way in which you can serve other people. Meeting the needs of other people has been the criterion for success for me. Finding a need and preparing yourself to be able to meet that need is the way to do something that you can be enthusiastic about.

Remember to pay attention to the way a person's nonverbal communication changes. Notice the changes and make sure that there is no miscommunication with regard to that. Ask if the person has any issues that have not been articulated. Vocally, verbally, and nonverbally pay attention to change and do your best to find out the antecedent to that change.

Our ability to communicate better will be enhanced as our knowledge of nonverbal behavior grows. The body language that a person portrays gives you some good insight as to how this individual perceives his relationship with you.

INTERVIEWING TIPS

Suggestions from a top New York City recruiting firm

Courtesy of: Sean Cronley, Partner and Richard Vogel, Partner

Charles Gabriel Partners, LLC
350 Madison Avenue
New York, NY 10017
www.charlesgabrielpartners.com

- Candidates must demonstrate enthusiasm during the interview. A perceived lack of interest is often the number one reason a candidate does not move forward in the process. Posture is important here. Being alert, attentive and engaging in a thoughtful and lively discussion is critical. Interviewers want to feel "wanted" and not as if it is a privilege to be interviewing you.

- Be sure to arrive at your interview early (5-10 minutes is acceptable) to allow you to get settled before meeting your interviewers. As Body Language states, an opinion is formed within the initial seconds of meeting someone so it is critical that you appear confident and in control. Appearing frazzled will be perceived negatively and demonstrates a lack of preparedness.

- If possible, do your best to find out who you will be meeting during your interviews. This will allow you to mentally prepare and to ask the appropriate questions to the appropriate individual.

- Find ways to break down barriers. If you are able to uncover a common denominator between you and your interviewer, (having previously worked at the same organization, having attended the same school, etc...) that will demonstrate interest not just in the opportunity but also in the individuals that you may be working closely with. Connecting on a different level may be viewed as a positive "differentiator" between you and others being interviewed.

- When you prepare your questions be sure to try and form them in a way that may allow you to discuss some of your strengths. You should always ask a question that allows for further discussion beyond just the answer. It is beneficial if you can get the interviewer to discuss a personal experience as a result. Ask position specific questions allowing you and the interviewer to remain focused on your ability to be successful in the role.

- Presentation is critical. Know your audience and be sure to dress appropriately. Take pride in your appearance and how you carry yourself during the interview. The firm is hiring a total package, not just what appears on the resume.

- Be sure to keep personal information to a minimum. It is common for an interviewer to take the first few minutes of an interview to ease in and discuss none job related items (how was your weekend, how is the weather, etc..). Be prepared for this but do not use it as an excuse to ramble about irrelevant information or worse yet, personal opinions.

- Answers to questions you are asked should be succinct and non tangential. Interviewers often view long winded and/or overly detailed responses to questions as a sign of nervousness and that the individual may lack a good understanding of what has been asked. In short, don't ramble.

- Follow the non-verbal cues of your interviewer. If he/she is warm and inviting than relax your posture as to not appear uptight or rigid. Conversely, if the interviewer appears stern then display yourself in way that is professionally confident and respectful. This is often a tact that is taken to see how you interact with positions of authority. Be cautious to never take an adversarial approach.

- Do not try and be something that you are not. Answer questions honestly and not how you think the interviewer "wants" you to respond. A skillful interviewer will pick up on this and will rule you out. While accentuating the positives, be sure to only answer questions honestly.

- Be sure to focus on the interviewer and the task at hand. Resist the urge to check your watch, cell phone, look out a window, etc....

MATTERS OF LIFE & DEATH
Body language use by the United States Army in Iraq

Jordan Brehove, a captain in the United States Army, was awarded two Bronze Stars for action in combat during his years of service in Iraq. He currently teaches military leadership at Massachusetts Institute of Technology and is pursuing graduate degrees at the Wharton School of the University of Pennsylvania and Harvard Kennedy School of Government.

On September 21, 2003, the second platoon of the Fifty-first Transportation Company was hauling military supplies in Iraq. A hidden roadside bomb unexpectedly hit the convoy while it was en route to Baghdad. U.S. soldiers had been attacked with deadly force, and it was time for action. The soldiers had to independently determine (1) who among the people walking on the outskirts of the town had attacked them, (2) who were the unwitting civilians, and (3) should they engage with deadly force—should they shoot and kill people? Reading the body language of individuals in the surrounding area assisted them in quickly answering these questions. The following are the ways body language helped these military service members make life and death decisions:

Proxemics and location
Because of the way roadside bombs are employed, a terrorist is always in a position to see the victim approaching and arm or trigger the device. So the quickest and most telling use of reading body language for a soldier is simply to see where people are positioned. A terrorist will want high ground with good visibility of the road but will be far enough away to avoid harm. So the soldiers will first look for potential terrorists in logical tactical positions. This is partly proxemics, as described in Chapter 11, but used at much larger distances.

Reaction
The explosion of a roadside bomb is shocking and intense even to the most war-hardened soldier, so the civilians in the area will certainly be affected. Some civilian Iraqis would flee, and others would take cover. These are natural reactions to the deafening sounds of a potentially deadly bomb, and these reactions could be considered the baseline. A third, and very suspicious, reaction would be to quietly observe the carnage or to actively seek a better vantage point to witness the activity. Such a response is not the normal reaction of any untrained person and suggests suspicious activity. You could say that this is not a normal baseline reaction for most people.

Cultural differences
Baselining is helpful to understand how a cultural difference may affect an assessment. Since we don't know every individual, we must first understand how local Iraqis typically act so that we know when something is amiss. For example, if you saw an Iraqi civilian squatting near the road before an explosion, you might think that the person had prior knowledge of the attack and was trying to avoid the blast effects by keeping a lower profile. However, a baseline of the cultural activity allowed trained soldiers to understand that it is common for locals in the region to simply stop and take a break by just squatting where they are; so the baseline tells us that this is not suspicious activity.

Military service members are highly trained and routinely briefed on recent intelligence so that they can respond to situations like the roadside bomb described here. But even with all that training, it is better to have more data points so that the military can be certain of its decisions, especially when those decisions mean life and death. Effectively reading body language augments the ability of these service members to make the right decisions at the most critical moments.

PHOTO CREDITS

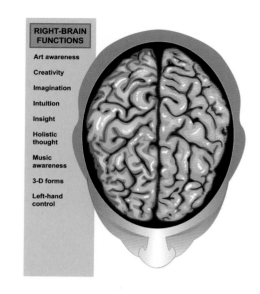

RIGHT-BRAIN FUNCTIONS

Art awareness

Creativity

Imagination

Intuition

Insight

Holistic thought

Music awareness

3-D forms

Left-hand control

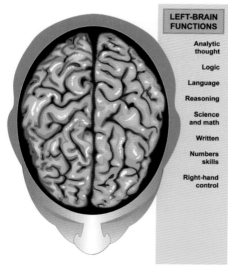

LEFT-BRAIN FUNCTIONS

Analytic thought

Logic

Language

Reasoning

Science and math

Written

Numbers skills

Right-hand control

GLOSSARY

Adaptor: This movement is typically an inadvertent gesture that helps people to relieve anxiety. It can be seen in the form of nervous ticks, clicking a pen, or self-touch gestures, such as rubbing the back of one's neck when stressed. There are also adaptors that do not have an underlying meaning aside from physical discomfort, such as an itch. This is one of five everyday areas of kinesics.

Affect Display: A movement of the face or body that reveals our emotional state. It should occur in parallel with other gestures or a fraction of a second earlier. Examples include laughter, smiling, frowning, or crying. This is one of five everyday areas of kinesics.

Anthropology: The study of human beings and their origins, including their evolutional, behavioral, cultural, and social development.

Baseline/Norm: A person's normal body language in any given situation. This is arguably the most important piece in understanding body language.

Chronemics: The study of the use of and perception of time in nonverbal communication.

Clusters: Groupings of communications signals and postures, verbal and nonverbal. These groupings aid in developing a more complete understanding of individual gestures.

Congruence: The level of agreement between various communication cues. A lack of congruence is commonly seen in deceptive people.

Deception: The act of willfully and purposefully misleading another. This includes the intentional omission of information.

Duchenne Smile: This is typically considered a genuine or joyful smile in which the corners of one's mouth are pulled up and

crow's-feet form around the eyes. It was first recognized by French physician Guillaume Duchenne in the mid-nineteenth century.

Duping Delight: This term, coined by Paul Ekman, describes when a person leaks happiness at an inappropriate time. We see this commonly in psychopaths who enjoy the sight of their horrific crimes. More innocently you can see this when someone is attempting to mislead a gullible friend.

Emblems: Culture-specific gestures that have a specific meaning. These gestures can stand alone and need no other signals or words to be understood. The extension of the middle finger is one of the more recognizable gestures of Westerners. This is one of five everyday areas of kinesics.

Gesture: A form of nonverbal communication relating to the movement or position of the body. This may be in place of or to support verbal communication.

Haptics: The science that deals with the sense of touch and how it is used in communication. Haptic preferences have been found to vary greatly across cultures. Haptics has outlined two varying types of communication, high context and low context.

Illustrators: Gestures to demonstrate or amplify speech that are used in conjunction with verbal communication. An example is showing the motion needed to shoot a basketball properly. This is one of five everyday areas of kinesics.

Kinesics: The study of gestures, facial expression, and body movement in communication. Five areas of kinesics used in everyday communication are emblems, illustrators, affect displays, regulators, and adaptors. Anthropologist Ray Birdwhistell coined the term in 1952.

Leakage: Accidental communication, significant in people attempting to fully conceal or suppress gestures.

Mammalian Brain/Limbic System/Paleomammalian Brain: The area of the brain that controls numerous functions including emotion, behavior, long-term memory, and olfaction (smell). This set of brain structures includes the amygdala, hippocampus, anterior thalamic nuclei, and limbic cortex.

Mirror Neurons: The neurons that give similar responses to performed and observed actions. These neurons were discovered accidentally by researchers at the University of Parma, Italy, studying what neurons fired when monkeys performed specific actions. It has been theorized that dysfunction with these neurons may underlie cognitive disorders such as autism.

Mirroring: The act of mimicking another person. Mirroring tends to aid in building rapport.

Neocortex/Human Brain: This part of the brain is responsible for higher order cognition and memory, including complex thought

and the ability to compute, analyze, critique, and create to an exter thought to be unique to humans. It is also the portion of the brai capable of lying.

Preening: To straighten, brush, clean, or primp oneself. In nonverb communication this can be done intentionally or inadvertently as social gesture.

Proxemics: The study of set measurable distances between peopl as they interact. Anthropologist Edward T. Hall coined the term i 1966.

Regulator: Anything used to control the flow and pace of an interac tion or conversation. Head movements such as nodding, eye move ments such as following along or looking away, or verbal response such as "yes" or "OK" to follow pace are all ways to influence pac

Raising your chin slightly or holding a finger up to cut into a conversation is another form of control. This is one of five everyday areas of kinesics.

Reptilian Brian/Brain Stem: This part of the brain is shared with reptiles and also controls heart rate, respiration, blood pressure, and digestion. Generally, this part of the brain controls any vital functions you do not think about.

Sociology: The study of the development, organization, classification, and function of human society.

Tells: A term commonly used in poker with the same meaning. It may be any action that reveals something about a subject and may be unique to a specific subject. These gestures may be overt or may be a fleeting microexpression lasting a fraction of a second. Tells individually do not typically have significant meaning, but a number of tells put together in a given situation will provide the viewer with insight into the intentions of the subject.

Triune Brain Theory: Model of evolution of the brain as formulated by Paul D. MacLean in the 1960s, which consists of three basic parts: the Reptilian Complex (basal ganglia), the Paleomammalian Complex (limbic system), and the Neomammalian Complex (neocortex).

INDEX

About the Author

Aaron Brehove is an author and television personality who has been a featured body language expert on the *Today Show,* CNN's *TruTv,* Nancy Grace's, *Swift Justice,* and has been interviewed by various print and electronic media. He has been a keynote speaker, jury and trial consultant, and fraud investigator who has been trained in interviewing techniques and detecting deception by government investigators from the ATF, FBI, and State Police. Aaron continues to work at one of the big-four accounting firms. His past investigations have included multi-billion dollar ponzi schemes, IRS tax evasions, and whistleblower allegations. He is also a senior instructor at the Body Language Institute, in Alexandria, Virginia. Aaron lives in Washington, DC. Visit him www.AaronBrehove.com.

About the Photographer

Roger Paperno currently resides in Seattle, Washington. His photography is simply gorgeous and fluid making him a perfect photographer for *Knack Body Language.* Roger has shot for Apple Computer, Chronicle Books, Clorox, Crystal Cruises, Norwegian Cruise Line, Royal Cruise Line, The Gap, Saturn Cars, Toyota, and many other cruise line and advertising firms.